THE INGLORIOUS YEARS

The Inglorious Years

THE COLLAPSE OF THE
INDUSTRIAL ORDER
AND THE RISE OF
DIGITAL SOCIETY

Daniel Cohen

Translated by Jane Marie Todd

PRINCETON UNIVERSITY PRESS

PRINCETON & OXFORD

Published by Princeton University Press
41 William Street, Princeton, New Jersey 08540
6 Oxford Street, Woodstock, Oxfordshire OX20 1TR

press.princeton.edu

Originally published as *Il faut dire que les temps ont change:
Chronique (fiévreuse) d'une mutation qui inquiète*
© Editions Albin Michel–Paris 2018

Library of Congress Cataloging-in-Publication Data

Names: Cohen, Daniel, 1953–author. | Todd, Jane Marie, 1957–translator.
Title: The inglorious years : the collapse of the industrial order and the rise of
    digital society / Daniel Cohen ; translated by Jane Marie Todd.
Other titles: Il faut dire que les temps ont changé. English.
Description: Princeton : Princeton University Press, [2021] | "Originally
    published as Il faut dire que les temps ont change: Chronique (fiévreuse)
    d'une mutation qui inquiète © Editions Albin Michel-Paris 2018." |
    Includes bibliographical references and index.
Identifiers: LCCN 2020052903 (print) | LCCN 2020052904 (ebook) |
    ISBN 9780691206158 (hardback) | ISBN 9780691222264 (ebook)
Subjects: LCSH: Social change—History—21st century. | Social change—
    History—20th century. | Information society.
Classification: LCC HM831 .C54413 2021 (print) | LCC HM831 (ebook) |
    DDC 303.48/33—dc23
LC record available at https://lccn.loc.gov/2020052903
LC ebook record available at https://lccn.loc.gov/2020052904

British Library Cataloging-in-Publication Data is available

Editorial: Hannah Paul and Josh Drake
Production Editorial: Karen Carter
Jacket/Cover Design: Michel Vrana
Production: Erin Suydam
Publicity: James Schneider and Kate Farquhar-Thomson

Jacket/Cover Credit: iStock

The translation of this book has been aided by Centre National du Livre

This book has been composed in Miller

Printed on acid-free paper. ∞

Printed in the United States of America

10 9 8 7 6 5 4 3 2 1

In Memory of Philippe

It must be said that times have changed
It's every man for himself nowadays.

        —DIANE TELL, "IF I WERE A MAN"

Time was not passing, it was turning in a circle.

        —GABRIEL GARCÍA MÁRQUEZ,
        A HUNDRED YEARS OF SOLITUDE

CONTENTS

PREFACE TO THE ENGLISH EDITION

IN THIS BOOK, I describe the transformation of economic structures and political thinking that has swept the world over the last fifty years, from the sixties to the present. The collapse of the old industrial society in favor of a digital society still in the making forms the heart of this account. By tragic coincidence, as the English language edition of this book was being prepared, the world was battered by a crisis unique in recent history, a pandemic, COVID-19. In a totally unpredictable manner, it served as a catalyst for a burgeoning of digital society, whose underlying logic, unexpectedly, it allows us to understand.

Because of the virus, society has suddenly become fearful of face-to-face contact. All of us are trying to protect ourselves from the risk of infection others may be carrying. Restaurants, cafés, and concert halls—essential sites where urban civilization can flourish—were closed. Life withdrew to the family cell, and the burden of stress and frustration followed. During the lockdown, every possible step was taken to allow people to work online easily, to purchase goods without having to physically enter a store, to entertain themselves without venturing out to a theater or concert hall. As it happens, the key feature of what can be called *digital capitalism* is precisely to reduce physical interactions, to dispense with the need for people to meet face-to-face. Under the assault of the health crisis, fine-tuning digital capitalism has come into the spotlight: increasing its efficiency by dispensing with the need to meet in person. Many activities have been rendered virtual. In medicine, for example, many consultations are now conducted remotely.

The big winners in the crisis were Amazon, Apple, and Net-flix, whose control of the market exploded during the lock-down. The virus arrived at just the right time for the domi-nant players in digital industries, who were able to conduct a full-scale experiment on the virtual world's assimilation of the physical world.

Back in 1948, the French economist Jean Fourastié pub-lished an analysis of long-term economic transformations which provides us with an essential key for understanding the change under way.[1] Fourastié announced that the "great hope of the twentieth century" was the transition from an indus-trial society to a service society. Human beings, he explained, had worked the earth for millennia and had worked materi-als for the last two centuries. In the service society, whose rise Fourastié was announcing, their work would be other human beings. His great hope was that humankind would finally become humanized in a social world where everyone would look after everyone else, as educator, caregiver, or personal coach. Fourastié nevertheless pointed out a problem which would have major repercussions: This service economy would produce much slower growth. If the commodity I sell is the time I spend with others, growth is by definition limited by the time available. This is known to economists as "Baumol's cost disease," a term coined by William Baumol and William Bowen.[2] Growth is necessarily kept in check when one has to meet in person, whether to examine the bodies of patients or attend a play. And the essence of capitalism, always and every-where, is to seek the systematic reduction of costs. It took a long time to find the solution to Baumol and Fourastié's prob-lem, but it is now clear: One has only to convert the humans we are, beings of flesh and spirit, into data sets, bits of infor-mation about our temperatures or our desires, so that we may become part of the Web, where we can be managed by algorithms. Freed from the imperative of encounters in the flesh, growth once again becomes possible—online.

During the spring of 2020, Paris, New York, London, and Milan stopped working. Health concerns became imperative, and was compared ironically by some to May '68, when the economy also suddenly came to a halt in opposition to the assembly-line work and mindlessness of industrial society. The comparison between the COVID-19 pandemic and the sixties is obviously comical. Back then, people threw themselves into the feverish pleasure of political demonstrations. Presently, COVID has us at home in lockdown, in a kind of internal exile. With the digitization of the world, the "great hope" that society would have finally been humanized is receding into the distance. In a strange inversion of May '68 values, it has been those on the right—supporters of Trump—who have waged the war against the lockdown in the name of freedom. The fact that a large number of society's loudest forces now bend towards the radical right is telling of the U-turn that our societies are engaged in. Yet the criticisms voiced by the young hippies in California and the leftists in Paris have also found echoes in present-day society, be it with radical groups such as Extinction Rebellion in the name of ecology or Black Lives Matter in favor of civil rights. The polarization of politics, the criticism of the contemporary world, are becoming as sharp as they were in the sixties, when they were directed against industrial society. History is coming full circle.

ACKNOWLEDGMENTS

ALL MY THANKS to guillaume Erner and Francis Wolff for their kind and indulgent reading of the manuscript; to Alexandre Wickham, faithful friend and editor, lifelong accomplice; to Richard Ducousset for his constant support of this project; and to Marie-Pierre Coste-Billon and her staff for their wonderful work on the text. I am also extremely thankful to Sara Caro for her early endorsement and to Hanna Paul for her thorough support of this adaptation of the French edition. Many thanks to Jane Mary Todd for her splendid translation and to Pamela Marquez for her final touches on the manuscript.

THE INGLORIOUS YEARS

Introduction

"THE TIMES THEY ARE A-CHANGIN'," sang Bob Dylan in 1964. And changed they have, but not in the way expected. Strange shifts have occurred, taking us from one world to another, totally alien from the one that brought it into existence. Hope for a bright future has given way to nostalgia for an idealized past. Populism has replaced leftism as the voice of protest. The enormous difficulty young people experience in imagining the future, their confinement to a kind of perpetual present, are the symptoms of traumas accumulated over the last half century.

The long, aimless wandering of the advanced societies has been the expression of a profound but undefinable discontent. Like an orphan who has inherited a fortune and who spends it in the futile hope of getting her parents back, postindustrial society has sought with all its might—but in vain—to reconnect with the old world's promises of progress. As if by the effect of a genetic mutation, a new, online species—all surface, without interiority—closer to hunter-gatherers than to farmers, has emerged: *Homo digitalis*, whose algorithmic life will decide the future of civilization. To understand the rage and frustrations that brought this *Homo digitalis* into being, to grasp also the carefree attitude and joie de vivre that have mingled with them, such are the goals to pursue if one wants to protect the humanistic values that are part of our heritage, before they are once again betrayed.

Fifty years ago, when this story began, the events that took place in Paris in May '68 ignited the imagination of its time in a way reminiscent of the French Revolution and its abolition of the ancien régime. For the young people who marched in the Latin Quarter, at issue was nothing less than to bring down bourgeois society. But, as Marx said, when history repeats itself, it often does so as farce.[1] May '68 was a joyous celebration; no one was guillotined. It was no longer a question of demanding bread but of "taking boundless pleasure" in an overabundance of riches. In Paris as in San Francisco and Berlin, a new generation thought it could create a new world, rid of the monotony of assembly-line work and material concerns, and composed of sex, drugs, and rock 'n' roll.

Unfortunately, economic growth stalled in the mid-seventies. A long period of stagnation began, shattering the aspirations of the sixties. The enthusiasm of a generation that had believed it possible to break free from the biblical curse of toil was shattered. This would be the first trauma of the past half-century.

The economic crisis soon offered the adversaries of sixties radicalism the opportunity for revenge. The Irishman Edmund Burke had blamed the French Revolution for triggering "discord" and "vice" and making the younger generations lose their "reason" and "virtue."[2] The neoconservatives, having returned in force in the early eighties, took up the same refrain. So the protesters of May '68 wanted to "forbid forbidding"? They were wrong: The existence of every society relies on rules and prohibitions. They wanted to "demand the impossible"? They had forgotten that the human condition is tragic. According to the critics of May '68, the "slide toward apathy, hedonism, and moral chaos" had to be arrested as soon as possible.[3]

In the eyes of those who voted for Ronald Reagan, his election exemplified the revenge of the reality principle over the pleasure principle. He was the standard-bearer of a moral as well as an economic revolution. Yet he would lend his support to an illusion just as naïve as that of the protesters, that of thinking that capitalism can regulate itself through a restored moral imperative. On the contrary, the world would witness the triumph of greed, his election being followed by an utterly indecent explosion of wealth inequality. The conservative revolution's betrayal would be the second great disillusionment of our time.

The transition from the sixties to the eighties might have been only an ordinary swing of the pendulum of human desire, from the wish for personal emancipation to the equally persistent need to return home to the warmth and coziness of one's own tradition.[4] A profoundly warped form of that opposition emerged over the last half a century. The joyous protest against the established order slid into competitive individualism, while the praise of tradition also underwent a transformation, veering toward the rejection of the traditions of others, toward xenophobia. In place of a (noble) confrontation between emancipation and tradition, we have witnessed a great schism between the winners—autonomous, emancipated from conventions—and the losers, seeking in tradition a protection it was unable to offer.

The rise of populism is the expression of that crisis. After an interminable odyssey in which the lower classes lost the frames of reference that industrial society had offered them, they are revolting against the Left, which is accused of moral laxity, and against the Right, guilty of thinking only of enriching

themselves. The migration of the working classes to the populist parties sounds the death knell of the hopes of a generation
that had written on the walls of its university buildings: "The
working class will take the banner of revolt from the students'
fragile hands." This is the third great lost illusion.

How are we to understand this series of crises and rup-
tures? What is the hidden pain of which this period was the
expression? The answer lies in a decisive factor: the collapse
of a civilization, that of the industrial world, and the enormous
difficulty advanced societies have had in finding a successor to
it. The idea of a postindustrial society, proposed to characterize our era, has catalyzed every sort of misunderstanding. The
Left interpreted it as the harbinger of the end of capitalism,
the Right as a return to its founding value, hard work. Both
were wrong. It is only in recent years that the veil has been
lifted to reveal its true meaning.

To understand the nature of the disillusionments that the
end of the industrial world has brought about, we must reread
Jean Fourastié's *Great Hope of the Twentieth Century*, a fundamental work published in 1948.[5] The hope of the new era,
according to that major economist, was that human beings,
having worked the soil in agrarian societies, then materials in
industrial society, would now concern themselves with other
human beings, in a society where work time would be dedicated to people rather than objects, in the fields of health, education, or leisure activities. It is that hope for a more human
economy that has been betrayed.

Fourastié underestimated the importance of one essential
point: the irresistible need for growth in modern societies. He
clearly acknowledged that a service society in which Mr. X
takes care of Ms. Y cannot grow. If the value of the service
that you sell is the time that you spend with your customer
(student or patient), growth must stall. Fourastié did not think

it would be a problem, but it did. The desire for growth has remained insatiable, however rich the advanced economies have become. It is possible, of course, "to work more to earn more," as a former president of France urged, but it would never be possible thereby to double one's earnings every fifteen years, the situation in the industrial world of the fifties and sixties. To enable an increase in purchasing power, economies of scale must be found that allow a service provider to take on a growing number of clients, like an actor who increases the size of his audience by moving from theater to television.

After a great deal of trial and error, it seems that postindustrial society has found a way to define and name itself: digital society. To achieve efficiency, everyone must enter the cybernetic world like a pill into a body, becoming a bit of data that can be processed by another bit of data. Software, artificial intelligence, will be able to take care of an unlimited number of clients, treat them, advise them, entertain them, provided they have been digitized beforehand. The prophetic film *Her* presents software with the capacity for emotion—whose bewitching voice is that of the actress Scarlett Johansson—in love with several million people at once. Such is the promise announced by *Homo digitalis*, that of a world emancipated from the limits of the human body.

The entire question is obviously whether the cure will be worse than the disease. Are robots going to replace humans and increase poverty? Will assembly-line work give way to efficiency protocols for the mind, via Facebook and Netflix? Through an extraordinary curvature of historical time, the old questions of the industrial world are arising in the heart of the world that replaced it. Do we have to pass through every stage of it once again, its moral bankruptcy and its financial crises? Can we do better? History is now being written, provided we do not err about its meaning.

PART I

Going Away,
Coming Back

CHAPTER ONE

Modern Mythologies

FOR THOSE WHO ARE NOW TWENTY, the sixties are as far away in space-time as the World War I was fifty years ago for their precursors. In both cases, the weight of the past is considerable. The young people reproached their parents for having forgotten the tragedies of history in the boring comfort of consumer society. The youth of today launch an accusation at their elders that is the exact opposite. It is the precariousness of the world, economic insecurity, that is now the object of reproach against their forerunners.

The critics of the counterculture of the sixties have accused the movement of being responsible for the contemporary world's sense of abandonment. The Woodstock crowd is said to have prepared the way for the rise of individualism and to have sown the seeds of economic liberalism. Thus, the San Francisco hippies and the young people who occupied the Odéon theater in Paris were working toward Wall Street's power grab? That is clearly completely idiotic. It was Reagan and Thatcher, the enemies of the sixties' protests, who twenty years later would discover an incredibly successful formula, pushing an ultraliberal agenda in economics under cover of achieving a moral restoration in the field of values.

The sixties were far more a critique of the growing individualism of its time than its cause.[1] Everywhere, whether in Berkeley, Paris, or Rome, young students expressed their anger against a society devoted to the cult of consumption. But for the economists who analyze that period, it looks like a true golden age. Growth was extraordinary, unemployment almost nonexistent. As Jean-Pierre Le Goff says in his memoirs: "Progress seemed finally to be fulfilling its promises: it was no longer put off as a bright future that could only be achieved through further sacrifices and efforts. It was becoming concrete in the present, through access to consumer goods and lifestyles that changed everyday life. The past seemed to be becoming obsolete."[2]

Under a veneer of opulence, however, a malaise was beginning to make itself felt. The newspaper *Le Monde*, in its edition of March 15, 1968, published a now-famous article by Pierre Viansson-Ponté, which perfectly summed up the torpor from which May '68 sought to wrest French society: "When France Gets Bored . . .". France, he explained, was at peace for the first time in a century. It had traded the heroic life for the comfort of bourgeois society. And it was bored! But Viansson-Ponté concluded, "for a people, that may be what we call happiness." It was that very happiness, the daily grind of *métro-boulot-dodo* (subway-work-sleep), that the young rejected. At both ends, in both production and consumption, industrial society was reaching its limits.

The world of production was that of assembly-line work, Taylor's organization of labor. Frederick Winslow Taylor's *Principles of Scientific Management*, written in the early twentieth century, remained the businessman's Bible. It brought the "stopwatch onto the shop floor," timing the average duration of each task to reduce it to the minimum. Under Taylor's influence, workers saw their activities reduced to a single, endlessly repeated gesture. Taylorism excludes laborers from the production process of which they are supposed to be the agents. They are excluded from the work itself: All the conditions necessary to perform the task are taken out of their hands. They are excluded from the realm of knowledge: the worker is not there to think. And they are denied control of their time: The pace of work and their breaks is predetermined. One exclusion sums up all the others: the worker is alone at his station, forbidden to communicate with others.[3]

Taylor was not unaware of the human tragedies that his system would engender. But he also surely thought that the workers, becoming richer thanks to the new productivity, would enjoy the fruits of prosperity outside work. Henry Ford, creator of the Ford automobile, grasped this very quickly. To tie workers to the boring work of the assembly line, he understood that he had to pay them as well as possible. There is a time to weep and a time to laugh.

It was this stark division at the root of the industrial world—work hard so as to be able to consume later—that became intolerable. Added to the fatigue of producing under dehumanizing conditions was an unexpected weariness with consumption itself. In 1957 Roland Barthes's cult book *Mythologies* had exposed with consummate humor consumer society's promise of achieving, under cover of emancipation, the petty bourgeois happiness of "calculation and order."[4] The first World Detergent Conference, held in Paris in 1954, had allowed him to comment with scathing glee on the success of the laundry soap Omo. "To say that Omo cleans in depth . . . is to assume that laundry is deep, which no one had previously thought, and this unquestionably results in exalting it, by establishing it as an object favorable to those obscure tendencies to enfold and caress which are found in any human body." Then, commenting on a new Citroën DS, the famous French luxury car, Barthes noted that it marked a change in automobile mythology. Previously paeans to power, the automobile was becoming "more *homely*, more attuned to this sublimation of the utensil which one also finds in the design of contemporary household equipment. The dashboard looks more like the working surface of a modern kitchen than the control-room of a factory: the slim panes of matt fluted metal, the small levers topped by a white ball, the very simple dials, the very discreteness of the nickel-work, all this signifies a kind of control exercised over motion, which is henceforth conceived as comfort rather than performance."

For the sociologist Jean Baudrillard, inspired by Barthes, consumer society is pervaded by a fundamental tension: it wants comfort *and* heroism. It is torn between "the passivity it entails and a social morality that for the most part remains that of action and sacrifice."[5] The way to resolve that contradiction, according to Baudrillard, is to dramatize life through the media. The consumer's tranquility in front of his television must be presented as a feat "wrested" from the turpitudes of the outside world. The violence of that world must be shown as crudely as possible, to allow the observer to savor the tranquility being offered. "Consumer society is experienced as a besieged Jerusalem, rich and threatened: that is its ideology. It is the ideology of the TV viewer relaxing in front of the horrors of the Vietnam War."

Fifteen years after May '68, the American economist Albert Hirschman, reconsidering Baudrillard's analysis, added an essential corrective.[6] In his eyes, the weariness of moderns in the face of consumer society must be understood as one of the consequences of prosperity. It is when the economic situation is good, when wealth exceeds expectations, that people believe they have had their fill of material riches. They then demand higher satisfactions; they want heroism, generosity. But prosperity is always relative. Whatever the level of wealth already achieved, the desire to consume, when it ceases to be satisfied, is quickly reignited. In periods of weak growth, the order of priorities is reversed. Crisis makes people selfish and leads them to turn inward. "Depression" can then be understood in both senses of the term, economic and psychological. Desire, according to Hirschman, runs counter to the economic cycle: it wants authenticity when growth is strong and material wealth in periods of recession. This theory would allow him to interpret the sixties and to anticipate the conservative revolution of the eighties that would follow, when the demand for "petty bourgeois comfort" would return in force, prompted by an economic crisis.[7]

Writing in 1978, Hirschman did not know that the sixties marked much more than the culmination of a growth phase. A far more fundamental upheaval was taking place: the fall of industrial society. Against all expectations, the trumpets of Jericho blown in 1968 would bring down the walls of the old fortress. The protesters that year obviously had nothing to do with its fall. They were more aware of the fragility of industrial society than they were responsible for its collapse. A totally unprecedented cycle was beginning, marked through and through by a loss of meaning. It would take fifty years to unfold.

Are Young People Bored?

The celebration of the fiftieth anniversary of May '68 made it possible for the French to relive, in pictures and as if in real time, that month of madness when France as a whole decided to stop working. Patrick Rotman gave a sober and precise account of "May '68 for those who did not live through it."[8] Strictly speaking, the Paris Spring began on May 3, with the first significant day of student demonstrations, and ended on June 30, 1968, with the legislature elections and the French people's departure on summer vacation. Viewed in terms of a decade, May '68 was situated halfway between the end of the Algerian War and the oil crisis of 1973. Decolonization was in full swing. The image of America, yesterday the liberator of Europe, had profoundly deteriorated. American support for Latin American dictatorships effaced the heroism of the generation that had defeated Nazism.[9] For young Americans themselves, the Vietnam War was the greatest abomination. Their loathing would extend beyond their country's borders. On February 17 and 18, 1968, a major demonstration against the war was held in Berlin. Daniel Cohn-Bendit, Alain Krivine, Henri Weber, and several hundred French people attended. In Germany, the leader of the student protest was Rudi Dutschke, known as Rudi the Red. Born in East Germany, he rejected both capitalism and communism. Following a vicious press campaign, he was the victim of an attempted murder. Two bullets to the head would leave him hovering between life and death for several days.[10]

In Paris, the spark ignited on March 21, when a Paris-Nanterre University student was accused of breaking the windows of the American Express office during a rally against the Vietnam War.[11] The next day, the university's administrative buildings were occupied. The March 22 movement was born. On May 2, Dean Grappin decided to close the campus after several classes were disrupted, including that of the historian René Rémond. The students left Paris-Nanterre for the Sorbonne, which would be closed in turn at the request of Dean Jean Roche. The May '68 movement was launched.

The police violated the immunity of the university and intervened. A night of street protests followed in Paris, on May 3. The movement spread to the provinces. In Toulouse, Lille, Bordeaux, and Marseille, thousands of students protested against police repression. Events reached the boiling point on the night of May 10: The students "occupied" the Latin Quarter in response to occupation of the Sorbonne. Paving stones were torn from the streets ("Under the paving stones, the beach" would be another famous May slogan), spontaneously, without planning. At two o'clock in the morning, the police mounted an assault: many would be wounded on both sides. The next day, the trade unions called for a general strike to be held on May 13. Ten years earlier to the day, in Algeria, demonstrations had led to the fall of the government and had precipitated De Gaulle's return. Ten years, a century, the general must have thought.

Working-class France joined the students. Work gradually came to a halt. In little more than a week, from May 14 to 25, the number of strikers reached ten million. The pro-China protestors brandished a banner that proclaimed: "The working class will take the banner of revolt from the students' fragile hands." On May 22 Dany Cohn-Bendit was expelled for declaring that the French flag should be ripped up and only the red flag kept. On the twenty-fourth, the students mobilized around the famous slogan "We are all German Jews."

On May 25 Prime Minister Georges Pompidou organized the response of the authorities. At the Ministry of Labor, he opened negotiations with the unions. The Confédération Générale du Travail (CGT; General Labor Confederation), perhaps encouraged by Moscow through the French Communist Party, played the negotiation game. At dawn on May 27, as another demonstration was being planned for the Charléty

stadium, with the support of the union's rivals in the Confédération Française Démocratique du Travail (CFDT; French
Democratic Federation of Labor) and supported by Pierre
Mendès France, a former French prime minister who ended
the French war in Vietnam, an agreement was hastily signed.
Wages were increased by 7 percent, the minimum wage by
35 percent, and union shops were recognized.

On May 29 de Gaulle vanished! He secretly met with General Massu, commander of the French forces in Germany. A
photo published by *Paris-Match* showed the president getting out of a helicopter, his face haggard, looking defeated. On
May 30, however, he took back the initiative. At the urging
of the prime minister, he announced the dissolution of the
National Assembly, while several hundred thousand demon-
strators marched up the Champs-Élysées in his support, the
novelist André Malraux in the lead. The strikes would last
another three weeks. Citroën reopened on June 24, Renault
on the twenty-seventh. In late June, the government won an
overwhelming majority in the Assembly. The gas pumps were
refilled. The French could leave for the weekend. The revolution was over.

SALUT LES COPAINS

The major factor that "explains" May '68 was the new demo-
graphic and sociological weight of young people. A third of
the French were under twenty at the time, outnumbering the
"old" (over sixty) two to one.[12] The number of university students had doubled since 1960 and quintupled since 1946. An
adolescent and dissident culture was emerging. The Beatles
and the Rolling Stones, born in English working-class neighborhoods, developed a home-grown version of the rock 'n'
roll that had appeared in the United Sates with Elvis Presley

and Chuck Berry. In France, Johnny Hallyday, Sylvie Vartan, Richard Anthony, and many others imported Anglo-American music, a "Dionysian frenzy, an explosive force," in the words of Edgar Morin, who would coin the expression *génération yéyé* (the "Yeah, Yeah" generation).[13] Rock, particularly its French version, expressed a new, carefree attitude that broke free of the old world of historical tragedy and political engagement. On a daily basis, adolescents looked forward to the broadcasts of the radio station *Salut les copains* (Greetings, Friends) and Radio Caroline, a pirate radio station transmitting from a boat outside British territorial waters.

For the sociologist Jean-Pierre Le Goff, "Youth was at the center of the transition from the old world to the new. Adolescence, experienced as a difficult passage from childhood to adulthood, reverberated in a France in the midst of change."[14] Young people's situation was unique in two ways. In the first place was the size of their cohort relative to the rest of the population. Everywhere, at the same time, the postwar years had triggered a desire for offspring, resulting in the baby boom. But it was outside the family home that young people met, at the high school, the university, or in the factories. In addition, this was the first generation to have been brought up by television, with programs specifically dedicated to the young. "Never trust anyone over 30," said Abbie Hoffman, one of the champions of the counterculture.

"French young people are bored," was Viansson-Ponté's diagnosis.[15] "Students demonstrate everywhere else, they're on the move. . . . They think that they have conquests to attempt, a protest to voice, or at least a sense of the absurd with which to counter the absurdity. French students worry whether Nanterre coeds . . . will have free access to the boys' dorm rooms." The journalist was alluding to another of the famous episodes that triggered May '68. On January 8, 1968,

Daniel Cohn-Bendit had shouted at François Missoffe, minister of Youth Affairs and Sports, who had come to inaugurate the swimming pool at Paris-Nanterre, criticizing him for not mentioning young people's sexuality in a report the ministry had just published. The minister had lightheartedly recommended that Cohn-Bendit jump into the pool if he had sexual problems.

What Viansson-Ponté was ridiculing was nevertheless one of the key questions raised by May '68: the outdated nature of the university system, its antiquated prohibitions, whether the segregation of men and women in the residence halls or the (entirely theoretical) exclusion of politics from university campuses. Girls were still wearing uniforms in the public schools. In the United States, women students had to leave college libraries at five in the evening. In France, the Neuwirth Law, allowing contraception, had just passed (with difficulty) in 1967. It was not until 1965 that wives could open bank accounts without asking permission from their husbands! Two centuries after the French Revolution, they were still under the guardianship of their husbands for most legal acts concerning them. For women, as for many social strata, the idea of autonomy, of freedom, remained a dead letter. For the sociologist Henri Mendras, who would speak of a "second French Revolution" between 1965 and 1985, "A chasm had opened between the law and mores."[16] Yet it was not until the seventies that women's liberation, especially the right to abortion, became a central question. As the historian Michelle Perrot would say, May '68 had to a large extent forgotten women and their distinct aspirations.[17]

An aspect of the protests specific to France, when compared to other countries, lay in the convergence of the struggles between students and young workers. Despite the French Communist Party's hostility to the "leftists," the two groups met. Ludivine Bantigny has calculated that, of the some eight-hundred people questioned by the police on the night of May 24, ninety-five were workers and more than sixty were technicians, from fitters to lab assistants, drivers to refrigeration mechanics.[18] Almost all were between eighteen and twenty-four years old. Thinking back on his own adolescence, Le Goff would comment nostalgically on this short-lived unity. "We have to put an end to the myth of the convergence between workers and students," he would say. "It did not go beyond contacts with unionized and politicized students, even though there was a sense of solidarity against police repression. But we had points in common. They were young workers who did not have much in common with the traditional image of the unionized and militant worker. They submitted to assembly-line work with a sense of being devalued. We were young students discovering a modern, impersonal university. Despite the differences in our social situations, we were all sort of young people in the new world, uprooted from small towns and rural areas."[19]

One of the major misunderstandings of May '68, which Le Goff brought to light perfectly in a book published in 1998, has to do with the role students assigned to themselves.[20] They dreamed of being the vanguard of the workers' movement, while the reality was almost the opposite: the young workers envied the students for their bourgeois adolescence. Christian Baudelot and Robert Establet have addressed that distinction.[21] For a long time, they explained, young workers had been leaving school to go work in the factories, while young bourgeois remained within the bosom of their families, went to university to learn to wield power. One side displayed "impatience to be an adult," while the other "was being initiated into the culture of the humanities."[22] These two social spaces did not communicate, but each of the two groups of young people possessed its own dignity. With the democratization of schooling, things became more complicated. A growing number of young people found they had no place in society, whereas previously they would have been at work. A zone of shared uncertainty was created.

The prolongation of schooling had an enormous impact during this period. It created the hope of social advancement among the newcomers, but it also led to disillusionment: The democratization of schooling produced a proletarianization of students, a loss of status. A text published in 1966 by the Situationist International, "On Poverty in the Student Environment,"[23] noted: "We can declare without great risk of error that students in France are, after police officers and priests, those most universally held in contempt."[24] According to the sociologist Pierre Bourdieu, the places of greatest revolt in May '68 were those where the mismatch between schooling and the labor market was highest, namely, in sociology or psychology departments. "Working-class intellectuals," Bourdieu added, "are unhappy and very dangerous people." Historically, they played a decisive role in the violence of the "Chinese cultural revolution, in medieval heresies, in the pre-Nazi and Nazi movements, and even in the French Revolution." Bourdieu spoke of a "lower-clergy resentment, always ready to rush into the slightest breach."[25]

It is clear, however, that the student revolt went deeper than a mere response to a dysfunction in the French university system. After all, it began on the campuses of the University of California, Berkeley and Columbia University and then extended to all the universities of Europe, including the London School of Economics, where Daniel Cohn-Bendit and Alain Geismar went to preach the good word. Even in the narrowly economic domain, it is not true that the generation of May '68 was a victim of the democratization of education.

According to sociologist Louis Chauvel's studies, the exact opposite was true. [26] Young people who were twenty in May '68 would have extraordinary futures, despite the crisis that later arose, even if they—naturally—would not know that until later on. Loss of class standing would affect the following generations, those that experienced the second wave of democratization in schooling, in the eighties. Éric Maurin conducted a statistical survey of those who graduated from French high schools in May '68.[27] The authorities, in the interest of peace, had generously awarded them diplomas at a rate close to 100 percent. Their careers were just as brilliant as those of other cohorts. The *baccalauréat*, the high school certificate, even when "tainted," favored the social ascent of those who possessed it.

But it was only in France that the student crisis of May '68 would lead to a political crisis. Gaullist France proved to be much more vulnerable politically than other industrial countries. "There's nothing between us and the communists," explained de Gaulle. May '68 rose up within the space of that "nothing," born of the need to assert a counterpower in the face of an undivided authority. The paradox of the Grenelle Agreements, signed in June between the government and representatives of the working classes, was that the unions would help the government transform into quantitative demands what was taking shape as a qualitative crisis. In raising the minimum wage and workers' wages, the Grenelle Agreements would attempt to translate into purchasing power the existential demands being expressed. What the CGT and Pompidou feared in different ways was that the students' idealistic exhilaration would spread to the workers. In a film, famous at the time, *Resumption of Work at the Wonder Factory*, a film by Jacques Willemot released after May 1968, we see a woman weeping in despair when she understands that the party is

over, that she must return to work, and that no wage increase
will ever reduce the suffering of her monotonous life.

Marx or Freud

May '68 was not monolithic. At least two different sensibilities
must be distinguished. To adopt a taxonomy proposed by Luc
Boltanski and Ève Chiapello, we can identify an "artistic critique" and a "social critique."[28] The first denounces consumer
society; the second, the mode of production. One revolts
against the hypocritical conventions of bourgeois society, especially in sexual matters. The other denounces factory life and
the exploitation of the workers. The social critique places its
hopes in the messianic role of the working class. The artistic critique wants to usher in a world in which the proletariat
would become unnecessary, because wealth would no longer
be material. What do they have in common?

The artistic critique was a revolt inspired by Rimbaud,
and the number of posters of the poet in the streets of Paris
equaled those of Che Guevara. This critique reproached the
bourgeoisie for fostering selfishness and opportunism. It contrasted the artist's disinterested creativity to the "proprietary"
lifestyle of consumer society. Boltanski and Chiapello note as
well that this critique shares with modernity its individuality. Stendhal, Flaubert, and Baudelaire, enemies of stupidity
and bourgeois materialism, loved Paris and hated the provinces, "the dwelling place of imbecility," said Flaubert. The
Situationists would be the principal instigators of this artistic critique (though they themselves pursued two conflicting
trends with respect to the social question). The occupation of
the Odéon theater under the slogan "The imagination is taking
power," would be one of their exploits. In 1967 Guy Debord,

their intellectual master, published a cult book, *The Society of the Spectacle*, in which he denounced capitalism as a mode of organizing social appearances such that everyone is assigned a fixed role in advance, as in theatrical productions.[29] In 1972 the Situationist International would ultimately announce its self-dissolution, fearing that "Situationism might come to constitute the last spectacular ideology of the revolution."

The other aspect of May '68 was fueled by a social critique of capitalism, the second term that Boltanski and Chiapello propose for understanding its inspiration. This critique adopted the Marxist denunciation of exploitation of the workers and announced the advent of a classless society. It drew its lexicon from Lenin's October Revolution and Mao's Cultural Revolution. Idealizing the greatness of the working class, some students went to work in factories. Robert Linhart, a former student at the École Normale Supérieure and a disciple of the philosopher Louis Althusser, wrote a famous book about his experience in a factory, *The Assembly Line*.[30] He would tell his daughter that he had gone to seek "the shining path that all the starving people in the world will take, all the peasants from the zone of darkness and storms." Virginie Linhart would herself produce a dramatic narrative of her life as a girl raised in the wake of May '68, torn between a leftist father and an artist mother: "With '68," she writes, "our parents thought that everything was possible. You could be accepted to Normale Sup at nineteen and be hired as an assembly-line worker at Citroën at twenty-four, like my father, to become an *établi*, to gain a foothold . . . My father never recovered from that time, when he believed it was possible to change the course of history."[31] The miracle of May '68 was that it marked the explosive meeting of these two critiques. One could challenge capitalism while being on the side of both the workers and the artists.[32]

In his book *The Cultural Contradictions of Capitalism* (1976), the American sociologist Daniel Bell analyzed capitalism as a permanent tension between the sphere of production, which is obsessed with the ideal of order and renunciation, and that of consumption, marketing, and advertising, which offers images of "glamour and sex, and promotes a hedonistic way of life." One sphere urges obedience, the other encourages fulfillment. There comes a time when they can no longer coexist. In Bell's mind, these "cultural contradictions" are heirs to the contradictions within the bourgeoisie, which wants to reconcile the moral order and the economic disorder that it itself produces,[33] and they replaced the economic contradictions that Marx placed at the center of his analysis. According to the author of *Das Kapital*, the proletariat had to remain poor, so that the bourgeoisie could get rich. It was necessary to get rid of capitalism to achieve the ideal of prosperity that capitalism promised. The "problem" was that the "Glorious Thirty," the thirty years of prosperity following World War II, demonstrated capitalism's unexpected capacity to enrich the workers. Discourses on proletarian poverty fell flat in a consumer society in full swing.

For the artistic critique, however, and contrary to Bell's analysis of it, it was the mindlessness of consumer society that was becoming intolerable, rather than its supposed appeals to freedom and fulfillment. The idea of cultural emancipation was a delusion, consumption being simply the flip side of assembly-line work, repetitive and boring. In the end, as Bell nevertheless concluded, it was more the dehumanization produced by industrial society than the pauperization of workers in the strict sense that was being denounced. The artistic critique and the social critique combined to reject standardization, the Taylorization of the industrial world, for both the producers and the consumers.

EROS AND CIVILIZATION

From one angle or the other, intellectuals quickly understood that they had to take Marxism back to the drawing board, complement it with new considerations on desire and sexual pleasure. As Vincent Descombes summed it up, "Marx had to be complemented by Freud."

Herbert Marcuse's *One-Dimensional Man*[34] and *Eros and Civilization*,[35] written by a sociologist transplanted from the Frankfurt School of Critical Theory to the University of California, San Diego, took on exactly that mission. So too did *The Sexual Revolution*, whose author, Wilhelm Reich, was a disciple of Freud himself. For Reich, sexual repression stood in the way of the revolutionary struggle.[36] According to Marcuse, Freud's idea that every civilization is condemned to repress instinctual needs, was historically out of date and could be left behind. A civilization without repression was possible, provided one knew how to reconcile "reason and instinct."

Marcuse's starting point was the Freudian theory that the sacrifice of the libido, of sexual desire, in favor of socially useful activities is the foundation of civilization. The victory of the reality principle transforms mental life through the development of the superego, by means of which individuals punish themselves for actions they did not commit. Are the pleasure principle and the reality principle necessarily irreconcilable, however? Marcuse noted, in the first place, that the power to control one's drives, to transform biological necessities into culturally constructed desires, increases satisfaction rather than diminishing it. A silent complicity therefore unites the two brothers, enemies in the mental life, the superego and the id, Freud's name for the source of all impulses. The sublimation of desires is not necessarily repressive.

Marcuse then noted that scarcity is one of the powerful mainsprings that ensures the triumph of the reality principle. Since society "has not means enough to support life for its members without work on their part, it must see to it that . . . their energies [are] directed away from sexual activities on to their work." With the development of the division of labor, "men do not live their own lives but fulfill pre-established functions. . . . Under the rule of the performance principle, body and mind are made into instruments of alienated labor." But "leisure," according to Marcuse, also obeys a logic of productivity: It must be "a re-creation of energy for work."

Nevertheless, the performance principle does not belong to the realm of necessity. With material prosperity (which, of course, comes as a result of that principle), the quantitative reduction of work time can lead to a qualitative modification of human existence. Marcuse's target here was the same as that of the artistic critique. It is consumer society and advertising that maintain the illusion of scarcity, of lack, within the society of abundance itself. Once one is liberated from them, "repressive reason gives way to a new *rationality of gratification*, in which reason and happiness converge." An alteration in "the relation between what is desirable and what is reasonable, between instinct and reason," then becomes possible. A "non-repressive sublimation" will replace the "repressive de-sublimation" of capitalism. According to Marcuse, repression lies at the foundation of bourgeois society, but material prosperity can make repression disappear.[37]

FRENCH THEORY

The parallel between "sexual repression" and "economic domination" proposed by Marcuse and Reich would constitute a large part of the intellectual foundations of May '68. The paradox of intellectual life at the time was that, in the eyes of the French intelligentsia, these ideas seemed much too naïve. As Vincent Descombes explains in *Modern French Philosophy* (*Le même et l'autre*), the linking sexual and social repression, which was central to "Freudo-Marxism," sounded like "a repetition of the foolishness of the eighteenth century: good nature, noble savage, bad society."[38] The paradox of the intellectual life of that period was that the great thinkers who were supposed to have influenced the protestors were in reality profoundly skeptical about the importance of the events.

Jacques Lacan, founder of the "Freudian School" and one of the master philosophers of the time, felt no indulgence toward the revolutionary romanticism of the protesters of '68. He shouted at the students at the brand-new Université de Vincennes: "I am antiprogressive. As revolutionaries, what you aspire to is a Master. You will have one." According to Lacan, "desire has its roots in the impossible, it is condemned to be satisfied only in dreams." Society, in issuing prohibitions, in reality placates individuals, by making them believe that the impossibility of their being satisfied comes from somewhere else. Lacan developed the paradox in these terms (I follow Descombes's exposition here): When a mother feeds her hungry child, she does more than satisfy a need. She offers him evidence of love. This results in an "inevitable" appearance of want, an insufficiency in the relationship. The mother can calm hunger and thirst, but no gift is sufficient to prove love.[39] The demand for love being bottomless, excessive on both sides, the mirage of an absolute object—the object of desire—arises to fill the gap thus created. But that object is a myth. It is the specter of a demand that is impossible to satisfy. No "sexual liberation" can do anything about it. The desire (for the desire) of the Other, with a capital *O*, remains forever insatiable.[40]

Lacan was one of the French intellectuals associated with structuralism. The structuralist method, inspired by linguistics, reinvigorated the analysis of societies by rejecting both Sartre's existentialism and Marx's materialism. One of its great thinkers was the anthropologist Claude Lévi-Strauss, who took inspiration from the approach of linguists to propose a new analysis of how societies function. "Linguistics," he wrote, "places us in the presence of a being external to consciousness and to the will. Language is human reason that has its reasons of which man knows nothing."[41]

What makes a society "hold together," without knowing it, according to Lévi-Strauss? The answer is its myths, which function on the scale of society in the same way that language functions for an individual: They make it possible to become part of a community. Hence, when a sick person feels an intolerable and incongruous suffering in the body, "a witchdoctor is given the task of resolving that disconnect between the individual's experience and the community's discourse. Through the appeal to myth, the shaman will place [the individual] back within a whole, where everything holds together."[42] As Descombes summarizes it, "Taming the brutal element of existence, assimilating the heterogenous, giving sense to the senseless, rationalizing the incongruous, in short, translating the other into the language of the same: that is where myths and ideologies operate."

What is the Western myth, analyzed in these terms, the one that holds modern society together, keeps it on its feet? For Lévi-Strauss, the answer is History with a capital *H*, which leads us to believe in a better future, or, at the very least, in the idea that history obeys a logic. In a famous chapter from *The Savage Mind*, in which he criticizes Sartre, Lévi-Strauss explains that moderns believe in history and the idea of progress, just as primitives believe in the eternal past. "For

Sartre," he explains, "history plays very precisely the role of a myth." It is necessary, he adds, "to challenge the identification of the notion of history with that of humanity. It is not because every person's individual identity lacks 'consistency' that human beings will recover the illusion of freedom on the collective level."[43]

The structuralists professed a "theoretical antihumanism," to borrow an expression from Louis Althusser, who proposed in their wake a new reading of Marx. For Lévi-Strauss, Foucault, Althusser, and Lacan, man is the product of structures that determine him, not the subject of his own action. Foucault characterized the individual as "the fictitious atom of an ideological representation of society."[44] Far from the optimism of Marcuse, who believed, at the end of industrial society, in an emancipation opening onto a unrepressive world, the French structuralists saw that eventuality as merely the last avatar of the Western myth of redemptive history.

SARTRE'S REVENGE

Structuralist thought, as Cornelius Castoriadis would summarize it, begins with the premise that men are helpless in the face of their own creations. This idea of "structures" that enclose the individual is vehemently reminiscent of industrial society itself and the rigorous division of labor that Taylorism imposed on its members. At the time, the idea that industrial society could shatter into pieces was unthinkable, even for the greatest minds. Questioned by Virginie Linhart about the generation of the protesters of '68, the architect Roland Castro responded: "They had a scientific passion for Marxism and they missed what surfaced in '68: the individual. They chained themselves to a mode of thought that had nothing to do with '68, whereas '68 was the individual unchained."[45]

In fact, May '68 marked the revenge of Sartre and his philosophy of freedom, rather than the intellectual triumph of Lévi-Strauss and Foucault. As Serge Audier has said, "in the events of May, in its unexpected and improvised aspect, there was something that exacted revenge for Sartre over Lévi-Strauss."[46] Sartre's analyses fit the demands of May "like a glove": "Loneliness, absence of communication, the sense of abandonment caused by consumer society," were central to Sartre's analysis, which saw the "coalesced group" of revolutionaries as the means to shatter that "seriality." Godard's films ultimately had a better sense of the atmosphere of the sixties than the scholarly works of Lévi-Strauss, Barthes, and Foucault. For Edgar Morin, Claude Lefort, and Cornelius Castoriadis, sympathetic commentators on May '68, "the ideals of autonomy and direct democracy" had to be interpreted as a critique of the "bureaucratic despotism and feudalism" that still structured society.

With the crumbling of industrial society beginning in the seventies, these philosophical quarrels would continue in a much more disturbing form. A long period of intellectual and political aimlessness was about to begin. What would be called, by default, the *postindustrial society* would have to elaborate a new "social imaginary"—to borrow Castoriadis's expression—in place of the old. To constitute that imaginary, a good number of new "mythologies" would draw from the lexicon invented in May '68. But it would be words, not objects, that would be recycled.

CHAPTER TWO

Lost Illusions (1/3)

MAY '68 MARKED a paradoxical moment. The advent of postmaterialist society was considered imminent, even as a crisis was brewing. The lean years were about to succeed the years of plenty. Despite a few worrisome signs, the five years following May '68 would continue to see very strong growth in France, more than 5 percent annually. In 1973 the French economy was still registering an astonishing growth rate of 6 percent. That would be the last prosperous year. By the mid-seventies, the advanced countries would all experience bitter disillusionment. The economist Paul Krugman would title his book characterizing that period *The Age of Diminished Expectations.* [1] Material prosperity, which had seemed assured, even excessive, was suddenly becoming uncertain. Like Proust's character Albertine, the growth of the Glorious Thirty would disappear, and no one would know how to get it back.

In October 1973, the Yom Kippur War between Egypt and Israel caused a spike in the price of oil when OPEC—the Organization of the Petroleum Exporting Countries—decided to reduce production. The advanced countries' economic growth abruptly collapsed, never to return to its former level.

At the time, it took a while to understand that the oil crisis in reality masked a profound rupture. The remarkable growth of the postwar years corresponded to a period when Europe caught up to the United States, as China is currently doing. Sooner or later, that growth had to stall, as Europe's standard of living converged with that of the United States. Yet few economists predicted that outcome at the time. The gains in productivity associated with the old regime of growth, based on mass production, were reaching their limits in the United States as well. The rationale associated with Fordism, which consisted of telling workers, "Work and you'll get a raise," was losing ground. As the economist Robert Gordon would later analyze it, the facts had to be faced: The dynamic of growth that went hand in hand with the spread of electricity and the internal combustion engine was reaching its end.[2]

To borrow John Kenneth Galbraith's formula in *The Affluent Society*, the Glorious Thirty were a period during which an increase in production stood in for redistribution.[3] Trade unions, more than governments, were the regulatory institutions of the system. When the crisis hit, working-class bastions, where the power of the unions was strongest, began to close one after another. The leadership of the working class was being eliminated. Séguin Island, on the outskirts of Paris, home of Renault and symbol of the workers' power, as well as the steel industry in Lorraine and the mines in the Nord department were shut down in the late seventies and in the eighties. Entire regions dedicated to industry, in Europe and the United States, would disappear. In France, the Nord region, home to the textile industry and coal mining, was bled dry by deindustrialization. In the United States, Michael Moore's film *Roger and Me* (named after Roger Smith, the head of General Motors), would depict his working-class hometown, Flint, Michigan, as a place devastated by the the automobile industry crisis. In Flint, the new hires were not factory workers but prison guards.

Deindustrialization is a complex phenomenon attributable to several factors in combination. Industry was in some sense a victim of its own success. Like agriculture before it, it was ultimately undermined by the very gains in productivity it generated. By reducing production costs, industry triggered a fall in prices, which at first worked in its favor. When cars or electronic watches become inexpensive, everyone can afford them. This tendency shored up demand and supported production. But when everyone has a car, when the rate of ownership is close to 100 percent, the rise in productivity makes hiring less necessary. Falling prices continue to stimulate demand, but less quickly than increases in production. According to Lionel Fontagné and Hervé Boulhol's study,[4] the tipping point at which that process begins to work against industrial jobs was reached in France in the sixties. Past that critical point, industry loses manpower in line with increases in productivity: The price effect that sustained demand for industrial goods no longer suffices to support employment. A study by Rowthorn and Ramaswamy obtained the same result for the United States.[5]

The decline of industry signaled that of the social world it had created in its image. In a manner that was rigid but also unifying, the society that vanished had bound corporate executives, engineers, and foremen to workers on the assembly line. Having exhausted the gains in productivity that electricity and the internal combustion engine had sparked, capitalism would have to reinvent itself. During the long period of uncertainties that began, the promise of wage increases gave way to the threat of layoffs and unemployment; the stick would replace the carrot.

Farewell to the Proletariat

The decline of industry would bring to an end the hopes placed in the working class, which the social critique had made the vanguard of world transformation. In France, François Mitterrand's election in 1981 had been driven by a simple idea, which Georges Séguy, secretary general of the CGT (the largest confederation of trade unions at the time), expressed: "When the steel industry has been nationalized, there will no longer be any reason to fear the loss of jobs in the sector, because workers will be protected like civil servants." But economic forces exist that are more powerful than the best intentions. Now in power, the Left reluctantly presided over the industrial crisis. Despite his campaign promise to save the steel industry, once Mitterand became president, he would have to resign himself to abandoning it. The French Left's troubles with factory workers date to that turning point.

With the rise of environmental concerns, the working class would also lose some of its aura among intellectuals. The contradiction between the artistic critique, with its yearning for a postmaterialist world, and the social critique, which asserted the primacy of the workers' movement, would become obvious. In 1980 the political ecology theorist André Gorz published *Farewell to the Proletariat*, which somewhat harshly denounced the earlier misunderstandings.[6] "The overcoming of capitalism, its negation in the name of a different rationality, will not come from the proletariat," he wrote. "The crisis of industrial systems does not herald a new world. No redemptive transcendence is inscribed within it."

Gorz's target was the Marxian analysis that the proletariat, by virtue of its very alienation, constitutes a revolutionary force. According to Marx, "The worker must be deprived of everything, so that his power as source of the world and of history may come to light."[7] Marx contrasted the situation of the worker to that of the artisan. Granted, the artisan is alienated when he sells the product of his labor—say, a pair of shoes—because the price and quantity of goods, dictated by the market, are entirely beyond his power. But when he is actually making the shoes, he remains in charge of production and can believe himself free. For Marx, it is precisely that limited, narrow autonomy that prevents the artisan, in contrast to the industrial proletarian, from achieving the universal. Gorz concludes that, in a freakish anomaly, "the ideology of the workers' movement perpetuates and, if need be, completes the work begun by capitalism: the destruction of the proletariat's capacity for autonomy. The negation of capitalism's negation of the laborer produces nothing positive."

According to Gorz, the development of capitalism has by no means heralded the development of a different form of rationality. Capitalism removed the desire or the power to reflect on the "true" needs of everyone, to debate with others the best means to satisfy them, and to define with complete autonomy the life choices that might be explored. "We need social experimentation," he concludes, "new ways of communal living, of consuming, producing, and cooperating. The alternative to the 'system' is neither a return to the domestic economy and village autarky nor the complete and centrally planned socialization of all activities. On the contrary, it consists of reducing to a minimum, in everyone's life, what must necessarily be done whether we like it or not, and of expanding autonomous activities as much as possible." That is exactly what was attempted by those who, in an effort to invent an authentic society without waiting for the revolution, chose a communal life. Their disillusionment would be just as great as those of the students who went to work in the factories.

The Pursuit of Happiness

The French newspaper *Libération* ran this classified ad in April 1971: "Live with others in authentic relationships, in a rural community in close contact with the urban setting, with other communities, and with neighbors, sustained by agricultural activity but also by anything you like (self-management). Collective responsibility and non-directive education of children in complete sexual freedom, using everyday life to challenge the foundations of a society we are fleeing: its alienations, hypocrisy, isolation, and poverty." Bernard Lacroix, who cites this ad in his probing book *Communitarian Utopia*, adds: "Above all, they know what they don't want—indoctrination, professional or partisan."[8] They were determined to live together, forging a life different from the one offered them by the society they were born into. Lacroix notes that no one anticipated "the risks of that collective life, that permanent tête-à-tête, men and women mingling together." But, he adds, who could blame them for the oversight?

As Roger-Pol Droit and Antoine Gallien write, "The month of May had given them the desire for something else; its failure disappointed them once and for all. Communal life became their only hope."[9] In the United States, the hippie movement, arising in great part from opposition to the Vietnam War, followed the same trajectory. A number of young people who had left to lead an "authentic" life on the margins of society would have a bitter experience of that world in isolation. In his confidences to Virginie Linhart, René Lévy, son of Benny Lévy—one of the leaders of the Gauche Prolétarienne (Proletarian Left)—would mention "the difficulty children have tolerating sexual freedom, the spectacle of adult nudity, of which we were the unwitting witnesses. The commune is not a good memory. These are my first memories of anxiety."[10]

Several obstacles would stand in the way on clearly marked road to happiness. In the first place, economic autarky turns out to be a difficult ideal to achieve . One must be able to pay for electricity, equipment, a vehicle. Several possibilities arise. For example, people can pool all or part of their financial resources. Those who go to work in the outside world must nevertheless work just as hard when they are at home as others in the commune. They must perform the household's chores, whether that means contributing to the maintenance of the community's "capital" (infrastructure, repairs) or to the collective labor specific to domestic life (cooking and so on).

Even love was called into question, along with everything else. According to one of the individuals quoted by Lacroix, "We never said we wanted to destroy the couple and the relationship between children and adults. We simply want to destroy the bourgeois—authoritarian and repressive—notion of the couple and the family."[11] Nevertheless, as a humorist put it, "The forms of association between a man, a woman, and a child are not very diverse in practice."[12] One must choose between free love and exclusive love. For many, this was no simple matter. Lacroix recounts the suffering of Marc when Yvonne stayed with Pierrot for four hours. "It was a rough shock for Marc. For ten years, he and Yvonne have been married and faithful to each other." "Marc was really hurt . . . No one is happy, and our relationships with the others are no longer the same," Yvonne would say. Marital choices swung back and forth between two poles: either the legally married couple continued as it was within the community, or group sex was introduced. A similar alternative arose in the case of children: Their upbringing was either the responsibility of the biological family, or it was truly collective.

Between these two poles, a continuum of situations would exist in the communes of the French protesters or the American hippies. At one extreme, a model of "weak communitarianism" would develop, where people earned their livelihood outside the community and where couples and "traditional" parental relationships were maintained. In such cases, the community simply offered a social framework for a shared existence. At the opposite extreme, a "communist" model would be implemented: There, total economic autarky and the socialization of children's upbringing reigned, and even sexuality was collective.

Very quickly, whichever model was chosen, the enthusiasm of summer gave way to the disappointment of winter. "Getting away, the great dream and the great refusal, tripping, it was great. . . . Sunshine, you know, with nice people: living in a groovy way, far from the city, without the constraint of going to work every day." One of them also wrote in his notebook on July 26, 1971: "The party last night surpassed anything you could experience or create collectively up to now, in its musical, gestural, and sexual intensity." But in the same diary, the tone of the entry dated January 19, 1972, was no longer the same: "It's very cold. . . . I'm not functioning anymore. I'm not made for a monk's life! . . . I have no desire to shut myself up with animals. . . . There are plenty of things to see elsewhere, and I don't want to cut myself off from them." After a while "it was as if the members of the commune knew one another too well to bear one another any longer." At the end of the road, only brawls or fistfights could settle practical disputes. "We're in isolation, cut off from everything else. For me, being cut off like that is a failure," confessed one of those interviewed by Roger-Pol Droit and Antoine Gallien.

It all began with a flight from the world to live in a collectivity. It all ended with a flight from the collectivity, which had become unlivable. How are we to compare this failure with the immemorial success of village or monastic communities? In reality, the village and the post-'68 commune have nothing in common. The first is defined by a past, its traditions and customs. The experience of being the object of the collective gaze is accepted by those who have known nothing else since their earliest childhood. By contrast, the commune remained an option for the members who constituted it. "Its founding character deprived it of the essential: duration, which is constitutive of social relations in the village."

The convent and the monastery show that it is possible to live according to such an ideal, even if one is not born into it. What is their secret? These communities are open, like those of '68, but young postulants must demonstrate their vocation beforehand. Whereas the village punishes deviants after the fact, the monastery stringently selects newcomers. According to Lacroix's analysis, "The commune is an unstable group that does not possess the effective means for carrying out its program." Its members can come and go as they please. They know they are free to leave.

The Children of the Dream

The kibbutz offers another example of a communal life founded on an ideal of authenticity. Upon their arrival between 1904 and 1914, the first immigrants to Palestine, fleeing the pogroms of the Russian Empire, dreamed of creating a new man, a "new Jew," and of restoring their dignity outside the ghetto. One of the pioneers was Aaron David Gordon, equally inspired by Tolstoy and by his faith in the virtues of country life. The psychoanalyst Bruno Bettelheim's *Children of the Dream* explores in depth the economic and psychological mainsprings of that communal adventure.[13]

In economic terms, the kibbutz is a radical revolution. Everything belongs to the community. Those who join give up everything they own and, if they leave, they take nothing with them. The kibbutz owes its prestige to the fact that it created a bulwark against adversity. The kibbutzniks became true defensive bastions, symbolized by the watchtower and the fence, emblematic of Zionist combat. Newcomers in the country illegally often managed to conceal themselves there. The ideal of pioneer life was also a reaction against traditional life. "The communal dining hall . . . serves as an expression of the deep rebellion against the old Jewish family structure, with particular reference to eating customs. The family meal in the Shtetl was a religio-pyschological sacrament. . . . The father sat at the head of the table and usually uttered the benediction; the mother spent a good part of her time in scrupulous food preparation; and the children, ranged around the table, witnessed the continuity of Jewish tradition." The kibbutz offered women the means to break free from these traditions, from the role written for them since childhood, that of the Jewish mother.[14]

But the years passed, even in the kibbutz. The "superego" of the pioneer in the face of adversity weakened once the War of Independence was won. The model of communal life broke down when the desire to distance oneself from ghetto life dwindled. The role of television, which played a role in privatizing lives everywhere, also ate away at the common space of the kibbutz. After performing their military service (which lasts three years), the young often went abroad and were not always inclined to return. The decision to pay for their higher education (which is very expensive in Israel) fell to the kibbutz, not the parents, who were increasingly frustrated by this situation.

To survive, kibbutzim have gradually become privatized, remunerating their members according to pay scales that reflect their qualifications and having them pay a growing share of the operating costs of the community (including the canteen). Today perhaps some sixty "traditional" kibbutzim survive. The others have been transformed into peri-urban residences. The children live under their parents' roof, the canteen charges for meals, and private property has been reintroduced. Most of the "children's houses," where mothers took their babies as soon as they were released from the maternity hospital, disappeared in the late eighties. The Begin government, supported by families arriving from northern Africa, cut off subsidies, calling residents of the kibbutzim "millionaires with swimming pools" and preferring to fund settlements on the West Bank. And, in the ultimate tragic irony, some kibbutzim were bankrupted by the financial speculation of their directors, who were duped by the naïve hope of solving their problems by investing in the stock market, which only accelerated their economic and moral decline.

Failure upon Failure

Ultimately, these experiments revealed the limits of the hippie illusion of a world based on the biblical simplicity of village communities. Firstly, the economic question turned out to be more complicated than anticipated. Being a farmer requires investments, materials, which necessitate engaging with the market and make economic autarky impossible. The solution often put into effect was to send members of the community out into the world, especially to developing countries, with the risk that they, like the immigrants themselves, would be unable to return. But another limit, this time of a cultural nature, also appeared. Moderns are not rooted in place. They need to play several roles—at home, at the factory, in bars—in short, to flee the limits of human existence by trying to live several lives at the same time. The limited space within which communes set the social existence of their members placed this experience of plurality in peril. It is a fundamental characteristic of modern societies, notes the American sociologist Erving Goffman, that individuals sleep, entertain themselves, and work in different places, with different partners, under different authorities, without that diversity being part of an overall plan.[15] Isolation in discrete communities destroys the possibility of playing these different roles. The absence of spaces or mechanisms that allow escape becomes burdensome. As Bernard Lacroix concludes, "From the outset, people gathered in closed communities are forced to learn a new form of sociability, characterized by false intimacy, ostentation, and enthusiasm, with no way out."[16]

The limitations of village life are too burdensome for young people who have experienced movies and television. The desire to pursue lives other than their own, to experience broader and more diverse communities emancipated from the physical and material limits of traditional communities, were aspirations that would shape the imaginings of the following generations, with the irrepressible irruption of "social networks."

Deadly Aberrations

On May 9, 1978, ten years almost to the day after the onset of May '68, the libertarian utopia swung in the direction of violence. On that day, the body of the Italian politician Aldo Moro was discovered in the trunk of a car. He had been kidnapped fifty-five days earlier by the Red Brigades, a Far Left organization calling for armed struggle. Moro, president of the Christian Democrats—the political party that had ruled Italy without interruption since the end of World War II—was the architect of what was to be the "historic compromise" between the Christian Democratic Party and the Italian Communist Party, representing the two most important forces of Italian political life, the Church and the Communist Party.

Leonardo Sciascia has written a moving text on this tragic episode of Italian political life[17]. He reprinted Moro's letters, which recount his expectations, his hopes, and the disillusionment he felt when he understood that his peers had abandoned him. This account plunges us into the confusion of the seventies, when the rage of May '68, having reached its limits, turned to deadly violence.[18]

During his captivity, Moro sent several letters: to the minister of the interior, the pope, and his friends in Parliament. These letters were met with unanimous rejection. The Italian state ruled out any compromise with the kidnappers. Pope Paul VI himself would dodge the question, simply calling on people to pray for President Moro.

The first letter Moro sent was the oddest, totally detached from the actual situation. It was addressed to his wife. "My very dear Noretta, On this Easter Day, I want to send you and everyone else my most fervent and affectionate wishes, with all my fondness for the family, the boy in particular. Remind Anna that I was supposed to have seen her today. I implore Agnese to keep you company at night. But I am doing fairly well, well fed and cared for attentively. I bless you, send you a thousand fond greetings, and give you a very big kiss. Aldo."[19]

Then came the letter to the minister of the Interior, Francesco Cossiga.

Dear Francesco, even as I address you an affectionate greeting, I am led by circumstances to lay out for you a few lucid and realistic considerations, taking into account your responsibilities (which I obviously respect). . . . The sacrifice of innocents in the name of an abstract principle of legality, when an indisputable state of necessity ought to commit one to saving them, is inadmissible. Every state in the world behaved in a positive manner [towards negotiations], except Israel and Germany, in the case of the Lorenz affair. And let it not be said the state is losing face because it could not prevent the kidnapping of a prominent personality who means something in the life of the state.

On March 18 a photograph of Moro arrived, holding in his hands a newspaper showing the date on which the photo was taken, with the Red Brigades flag in the background. Moro appeared in the photo with the same expression of "weariness, languor, and that spark of irony within a fog of boredom. . . . Between the eyes and lips, you glimpsed of a spark of irony or contempt, but immediately veiled by that weariness, that boredom. There are centuries of sirocco, it was said, in his gaze. . . . He is the personification of southern pessimism," of the conviction that "every thing, every idea, every illusion—even the ideas and illusions that seem to make the world go round—is speeding toward death: except thinking about death, the idea of death, which for its part never dies."

No response was forthcoming. The Red Brigades issued an ultimatum. "The release of the prisoner Aldo Moro cannot be considered except in exchange for the release of the Communist prisoners. A clear and definitive response is expected within forty-eight hours." Moro understood that his fate was sealed. After the deadline had passed, he composed a last letter: "I request that neither the state authorities nor the party leaders participate at my funeral. I ask that I may be followed by the few people who truly loved me and who are therefore worthy of accompanying me with their prayers and love."

The Rise of Violence

Moro's assassination marked the height of political violence in Italy. The deadly decade of the seventies has been called the *Anni di piombo*, the "Years of Lead." They culminated in—but were not limited to—Moro's assassination. Several other tragic events followed one after another, such as the attack on the train station in Bologna in 1980 by Far Right militants, which would kill eighty-five and wound more than 200. The Far Left, for its part, repeatedly aimed machine-gun fire at the legs of personalities it wanted to intimidate.

Germany, Italy, and Japan, the three Axis powers, were the places where post–May '68 violence was the worst. Henri Weber notes that the conflict between parents and children was most intense in these three countries.[20] For the most part, France escaped the rise of radical violence that seized hold of Italy. The group Action Directe was an exception. It was responsible for the assassination of two major figures: General Audran, head of procurement at the Ministry of Defense; and Georges Besse, the CEO of Renault (the members of Action Direct apparently intended to run through the alphabet). For Hervé Rotman, outbursts of violence were ultimately avoided in France because "The group in charge of the Gauche Prolétarienne decided to put an end to an organization that was only inches away from shifting from symbolic—but very real—violence to armed violence. I believe that, for months, its leaders carried out an educational campaign to prevent militants from drifting into irreparable action. . . . The most powerful Far Left groups, Krivine's Ligue Communiste [Révolutionnaire] and Benny Lévy's Gauche Prolétarienne, channeled and held back spontaneous and individual violence that might have been expressed through the use of arms."[21]

The political violence that arose in the advanced countries was not limited to leftist groups straying into deadly ideology. The violence was only the shadow cast by a much more widespread phenomenon. Throughout the sixties and seventies, the number of homicides exploded in most of the wealthy countries, increasing by a factor of 2.5 in the United States and Europe. Canada followed the same trend, though it began at a lower level. The comparison between Canada and the United States is enlightening. Canada has only one-third the homicides of the United States, where violence is partly an inheritance of the South—racist and violent—and the settlement of the West by lawless cowboys. Historically, Canada has been much less violent, because the Mounted Police pacified the frontier before the settlers moved in. Nevertheless, over the course of the sixties, Canada was subject to the same increase in violent acts as the United States.

Steven Pinker, a professor of psychology at Harvard, has adopted the analyses of the sociologist Norbert Elias to place that evolution in perspective. According to Elias, a "civilizing process" got under way in Europe in the seventeenth century and would gradually eradicate personal violence. In *The Better Angels of Our Nature*, Pinker shows that European criminality is presently one-fiftieth of levels of the seventeenth century.[22] It was in the seventeenth century that the Wars of Religion reached their height on the European continent. After the atrocities committed during this period, the state finally acquired a "monopoly on legitimate violence" for a population exhausted by wars and murders. Acts of violence would not disappear, however. As Robert Muchembled has shown, they would gradually migrate from one front to another, toward domestic violence on the one hand and "legitimate" wars against foreign countries on the other. The state would be cured of that martial violence only much later.[23]

Why did civil violence grow to such an extent in the sixties? According to Pinker, a "de-civilizing" process was set in motion during this period. A regression took place in self-control, in the taming of passions that had been central to the process Elias described. The praise of spontaneity and the denunciation of bourgeois morals were part of the credo of the time. At the start of the film *Easy Rider*, Peter Fonda and Dennis

Hopper pointedly throw away their watches. And the rock group Chicago Transit Authority sang: "Does anybody really know what time it is? Does anybody really care?"[24] Spontaneity, the denunciation of inhibitions, and the praise of passions became cardinal virtues. Bob Dylan wrote: "Well, I try my best / To be just like I am / But everybody wants you / To be just like them." Jerry Rubin, an American counterculture leader of the time, published a book titled *Do It*.[25] According to the sociologist Cas Wouters, a culture of informality was replacing the norms of bourgeois society.[26] Drug use, which increased exponentially, also contributed to the rise of violence, fueled by the criminality that flourished in the drug culture.[27]

Just as the Reign of Terror under Robespierre derailed the French Revolution, the criminal violence of the seventies ultimately ruined the counterculture of the sixties. In part, it was this violence that would trigger the conservative counter-revolution, heralded as a return to moral order as much as a solution to the economic crisis. It would not be until the eighties that the level of violence would once again drop, but not because of the conservative revolution.

CHAPTER THREE

The Conservative Revolution

THE 1979 FILM *The Deer Hunter,* directed by Michael Cimino, marked its era with a brutal depiction of the Vietnam War never before been seen in war films. The young recruits are subjected to unbearable cruelty, obliged to play Russian roulette in a prison camp. And yet, at the end of the film, the group of friends devastated by the war has a reunion at a restaurant after the funeral of one of its members. While preparing an omelet, the chef whistles the national anthem. All of them sing along. The patriotism of these young men, the children of Russian immigrants, is intact. The film ends with a toast to Nick, the friend who has died, the one who went through psychological and moral hell. The film was interpreted as heralding the conservative revolution.

Reagan's political victory was achieved thanks to the support of American blue-collar workers, like the factory workers depicted in the film, who remained patriotic to the very end. This implausible phenomenon, which the Democratic Left had not foreseen, would be replicated everywhere in the world. The American sociologist Christopher Lasch wrote an overview of the movement titled *The True and Only Heaven: Progress and Its Critics*, whose starting point was to understand "The unexpected resurgence of the right, not only in the United States but throughout much of the Western world." He writes, "Who would have predicted . . . that as the twentieth century approached its end, it would be the left that was everywhere in retreat?" "The course of history favored the left," he continues, everyone had thought that "some form of socialism, at the very least a more vigorous form of the welfare state, would soon replace free-market capitalism."

The New Right came to power, he adds, with a mandate "not just to free the market from bureaucratic interference but to halt the slide into apathy, hedonism, and moral chaos." Indirectly adopting André Gorz's ideas, Lasch explains that the working class had not at all embraced the Marxist idea that the salvation of the proletariat required that it be transformed into generalized labor in the factories. What interested the working classes was the dream of an independent existence as artisans or peasants, a certain autonomy, however partial it might be. This refusal to vanish into the proletarian universality vaunted by Marx explains why blue-collar workers would rally behind Reagan's program. Like ancien régime peasants who dreamed of owning their lands, the working classes aspired to leave behind their condition as wage laborers and set up their own businesses.

Twenty years after the young and handsome John F. Kennedy, a Christ figure for progressive America, was elected president, the retired actor Reagan returned to take center stage in an America in decline. Kennedy had taken office in the country's golden age. The indicators of American well-being had risen to levels they would never see again. In 1964 Reagan had supported the candidacy of Barry Goldwater, a Far-Right candidate who received only 39 percent of the vote. Twenty years later, the old actor reappeared at the height of the crisis. The country was bogged down in inflation and unemployment. The Vietnam War had plunged Americans into the depths of moral despair. The film *Taxi Driver* (which, like *The Deer Hunter*, starred Robert De Niro) captures that moment of extreme tension, when meaninglessness pervaded America. "Are the good times really over for good? It was back when the country was strong . . . Before the Vietnam war came along."

Reagan's strength lay in combining in a single bloc the (white) working classes and the Wall Street elites. He united his followers around a simple idea: Work is salvation. As Nicolas Sarkozy would say twenty years later, one must "work more to earn more." Those who do not work hard are the victims of their own indigence. Opposing the welfare state head-on, Reagan denounced assistance to the poor as the real cause of their poverty. Everyone in the United States understood that by "poor" he meant "Black."

The essayist Guy Sorman, one of the standard-bearers of the conservative revolution in France, paraphrases the conservative thinker Allen Matusow: "Why are 40 percent of young Blacks unemployed when, every year, a thousand Asian, Hispanic, and Caribbean immigrants find a place in the economic system without great difficulty?" [1] Analyzing the history of Black Americans, Thomas Sowell, himself African American, claimed that Blacks climb the social ladder by the same means as the other races.[2] Sowell notes, as Olivier Roy would do much later regarding the jihadists, that the second generation is the most tempted to commit violence, because it is cut off from its roots and not yet integrated into the middle class. Hence gangs were made up predominantly of American Jews in the twenties, and later of Italians. Now they are made up of Blacks. And he concludes: Anti-Semitism did not prevent the Jews from getting rich, why would racism prevent the Blacks from doing so as well?

Thomas Sowell and Walter Williams drew the conclusion that affirmative action for Blacks had to be abandoned for their own good. According to these writers, the welfare state makes poverty tolerable and thus sustains it rather than making it disappear. In this regard, neoliberalism took on the accents of the early nineteenth century, when the English Poor Laws were denounced with the same arguments.[3] According to George Gilder, "public assistance pushes Blacks into an untethered life, as they wait for the green tide of welfare checks."[4]

In *Losing Ground*, Charles Murray would add another layer to that argument: public assistance leads to "moral degeneracy." Murray proposes that, after the "debaucheries of the sixties," it was necessary to restore the Puritan values of heartland America: work, self-denial, and the patriarchal family. He adopts Gilder's view that the household anarchy of the poor on social assistance inhibits the desire to work, disunites the family, and erodes religious fervor. Murray goes even further in *The Bell Curve*, written with Richard Herrnstein.[5] He puts forward the idea that schooling does not benefit the poor, because their IQ is too low to allow them to learn. Fortunately, several studies would deflate such absurd claims. A study on education by Orley Ashenfelter, for example, shows that IQ absolutely cannot predict the benefit a given student will draw from the educational system.[6] Murray also claims that the poorer nations are the victims of the low IQ of their residents, as are the poor themselves in wealthy countries. Yet Australia, one of the countries that is now among the wealthiest in the world and one of the most peaceful, was originally populated by ex-convicts from Victorian England. A theory of poverty based on IQ and heredity would have difficulty explaining that tremendous change in status.

One of the forms that hatred of the federal government takes is a rejection of the welfare state, which is nothing new.

It is a constant in American history, but the economic crisis gave it new intensity. The movement Franklin Roosevelt launched in the thirties to create a protective and far-sighted state began to change direction. In the eyes of neoconservative thinkers such as Irving Kristol, the New Deal primarily benefited intellectuals, professors, and social workers, who in reality turned the welfare state to their own advantage. These thinkers scorned the American middle class's values: hard work, discipline, morality, thrift, ownership.

In fiscal matters, the hostility towards government was brewing in the seventies. It began in California, which in 1973 passed Proposition 13, a measure that sharply reduced property taxes. It was during this period that the economist Arthur Laffer drew, on a napkin in a San Francisco restaurant, a curve based not on science but solely on the author's chutzpah. With a tax rate of 0 percent, a state earns nothing. But at a rate of 100 percent, it also earns nothing, since no one is motivated to work. Tax revenues thus resemble an inverted U. They rise and fall in accordance with the tax system: Too much taxation obliterates tax revenues. This theory would provide one of the arguments that allowed Reagan to lower the income tax by 25 percent, leading to a huge federal deficit. The theory in vogue under Reagan's tenure would be "trickle-down economics." The rich must be allowed to grow richer, and the poor will receive a greater benefit from that process than they would from receiving tax subsidies.

The Betrayal of the Enlightenment

The success of Reagan's programs—which combined economic neoliberalism and moral conservatism—among the working classes would be a decisive tipping point in the political history of the last half-century. It would reach far beyond the United States and Margaret Thatcher's England. The Israeli sociologist Eva Illouz, for example, notes the remarkable parallel between Reagan's election and Menachem Begin's coming to power in Israel two years earlier.[7]

The Israel of the early pioneers was composed of Ashkenazi Jews, who had arrived from Russia and Poland before and after World War II. According to Illouz, they would welcome the Sephardic Jews from North Africa—the *mizrahim*, as they were called—with the same "solicitude" with which the French welcomed immigrant workers during the Glorious Thirty. "The Ashkenazi Zionists restricted the *mizrahim* to lowly jobs, with the men working as truck drivers, lumberjacks, and laborers, and the women as domestic or factory workers." The *mizrahim* were considered "primitives." Even their religiosity became a mark of cultural inferiority vis-à-vis the Ashkenazi, who made secularism the banner of modernity.

Begin made an appeal to the *mizrahim* in order to fight the Labor Party, considering their faith a positive value. The same paradox as in Reagan's America played itself out: Even as the Likud liberalized the economy and persisted in privileging the rich, the *mizrahim*, economically speaking the victims of that liberal policy, never stopped supporting him, because he acknowledged their "Israeli identity as Jews." The same pattern would be evident everywhere. In *The Enlightenment on Trial*, Daniel Linderberg notes that the return of Hindutva in India fit the same mold, combining faith and capitalism.[8] Irving Kristol, a leading American conservatives, summed up the program of neoconservatism in its many iterations with the triptych "religion, nationalism, and economic growth."[9]

CYCLES OF MORALITY

The return of conservative thought in the eighties, so soon after the sixties had given voice to ideas diametrically opposed to it, came as a huge surprise to observers. That pendulum swing was not unprecedented, however. At the turn of the eighteenth century, after the waters of the French Revolution had receded, the same opposition to progressive ideas arose. Before the Revolution, the Enlightenment had championed the ideals of autonomy and freedom, in somewhat the same way that Godard and Truffaut anticipated May '68. But then came the backlash of the Thermidorian Reaction, and, after the fall of Napoleon, Metternich's return to Vienna and the restoration of the monarchy in France.

The philosopher Robert Legros shows why this swing of the pendulum can be interpreted as a characteristic feature of the modern world. European thought, he explains, has since the eighteenth century been erected on the idea that there is no "human nature" in the sense that animals have a fixed nature. Man is what he wants to become. But from the same starting point, two radically different sets of implications were drawn. For the Enlightenment philosophers, man becomes authentically himself by "breaking free" of cultural or religious traditions, tearing off the mantle of social conventions. For Kant, the idea underlying Enlightenment goals is to bring humanity into adulthood, to make it capable of thinking, acting, and judging for itself: It is in submitting to a religion, to practices and mores, habits and customs, in short, to tradition, that the individual renounces his original autonomy.

For the Romantics who followed in the history of ideas it was in reality the Enlightenment program that was dehumanizing. When the "autonomy" vaunted by the Enlightenment is an end in itself, it becomes pointless. It leads only to a search for artificial needs to satisfy, needs that man comes to believe are "natural" but which in fact drag him down to the level of animals. Because there is no human nature, the Romantics continue, humanity exists only in the particular civilizations, religions, and languages it has created. The act of breaking free—of withdrawing from any particular humanity—is a form of alienation.

Romanticism also encourages the notion that the universal is achieved only through particularization. Abstract universality is an empty universality. The reactionary thinker Joseph de Maistre summed it up in 1795 with these words: "In my life I have seen Frenchmen, Italians, Russians; thanks to Montesquieu, I even know that it is possible to be Persian; but as for man, I declare I have never met him in my life."[10] Almost two-hundred years later, Christopher Lasch, commenting on the Reagan revolution, took up this argument in almost identical terms: "The capacity for loyalty . . . needs to attach itself to specific places and not to an abstract ideal of universal human rights. We love particular men and women, not humanity in general. The dream of universal brotherhood, because it rests on the sentimental fiction that men and women are all the same, cannot survive the discovery that they differ."[11]

The neoconservatives who prospered in the eighties cast themselves perfectly in the mold of that tradition, appropriating Joseph de Maistre's program of "combatting the Enlightenment with the Enlightenment's weapons." Christopher Lasch, quoting Lewis Mumford, adds that "societies based on progressive principles . . . renounced every larger goal in favor of the 'private enjoyment of life.'" Denying that life has any other meaning, or value, or possibility, he writes, "Advocating ideals of individualism, social mobility, and self-realization that come closest to fulfillment in the professional classes, liberals defended the underdog in an upper-class accent." He contrasts this modern apathy to "virtue" (among the ancients) and "grace" (among the Christians), which "enabled men to live undespairingly with the knowledge of finitude, the poignant contrast between the absolute and the contingent."[12]

The American Allan Bloom rode the success of the conservative revolution with a book that would become a best seller: *The Closing of the American Mind* (1987).[13] Describing the situation of young Americans in the sixties, when he himself began to teach, Bloom portrays them as young people who "have never experienced the anxieties about simple physical well-being that their parents experienced during the depression. They have been raised in comfort and with the expectation of ever increasing comfort." The students' souls, he adds, are "exhausted and flaccid, capable of calculating, but not of passionate insight." "The delicate fabric of civilization, made of the woof and warp of successive generations, has come completely unraveled, and the children are raised but not educated."[14] According to Bloom, parents continued to devote the better part of their lives to their offspring. But, he argued, the family "has to be a sacred unity believing in the permanence of what it teaches, if its ritual and ceremony are to express and transmit the wonder of the moral law, which it alone is capable of transmitting and which makes it special in a world devoted to the humanly, all too humanly, useful."

As Legros notes, the political paradox of the "romantic" counterrevolution is that, while it brought about a subversion in the philosophical realm, it tended to embrace a radical conservatism on the political level. It is obliged to believe that the only legitimate attitude of modern man is to submit to his own tradition. For example, Edmund Burke contrasts the French Revolution to the English model, where liberties are "an entailed inheritance derived to us from our forefathers, and to be transmitted to our posterity."[15] Romanticism is a critique of the Enlightenment, but it is permissible to see the Enlightenment as an (anticipated) critique of Romanticism. To take civilizations as man's "natural" element is to close your eyes to the fact that these civilizations did not make themselves. To recognize their authority in advance is to deny man's freedom vis-à-vis what he has created. The swing back and forth from the desire to break free and the need to establish roots is never-ending. No synthesis is possible. It is necessary to try one, then the other, ad infinitum.

In combining Legros's and Hirschmann's theories, we can draw up one moral type for the sixties, which emerged when growth was strong and the desire for emancipation found expression, and another for the eighties, when the economic recession triggered the moral need for traditions and protections. Despite the hopes spurred by the return of growth in the nineties, a profoundly altered version of that oscillation was set in motion at the time. The left to right pendulum would swing even farther to the right, the far right.

Kondratiev Mon Amour

(LOST ILLUSIONS, 2/3)

The conservative revolution was set off in great part by the crisis of the seventies. Growth returned two decades later, around the mid-nineties, again brightening the landscape of the advanced countries. Optimism was reborn! Two million jobs were created in France between 1997 and 2000. Articles proliferated in the United States extolling the miracle of what was called "the new economy" based on computer and communications technologies.[16]

For many commentators, a new "Kondratiev wave" was emerging. Nikolai Kondratiev was director of a statistics thinktank in Moscow when he wrote his fundamental article in 1923, which was translated into English in 1928.[17] In his major study *Business Cycles*, Joseph Schumpeter coined the expression "Kondratiev waves" to characterize the economy's propensity to move in cycles of about fifty years. In his terminology, phase A of the cycle is characterized by a growth period, phase B by recession (or at least a pace of growth significantly slower than that of phase A). Each phase lasts about twenty-five years.

The Kondratiev waves created the sense that a metronomic regularity was at work between the peak phases of economic activity and the troughs. For instance, the peak phase extended from 1948 to 1973, the trough from 1974 to 1997. A century earlier, according to Kondratiev's research, there had been a growth phase during the period 1849–1873. It was followed by a major recession from 1873 to 1897, then a new growth phase from 1898 to 1923. And, in the preceding century, phase A extended from 1790 to 1814, followed by a (slightly longer) trough from 1814 to 1848. For Kondratiev's followers, no doubt was possible: In 1998 a new cycle of growth was beginning, destined to last until the mid-2020s. Each of the previous cycles had been linked to the diffusion of new technologies: the power loom, the railroad, electricity. This one would be the computer wave.

A new cycle also seemed to be beginning in the political realm. Thatcher was replaced by Tony Blair, Reagan by Bill Clinton. In France, the socialist Lionel Jospin was named prime minister. A peak cycle in Legros-Hirschman's sense was being set in place. When prosperity returned, the need for financial security eased, and a desire for emancipation resurfaced. The divorce rate, for example, increases with economic growth. According to a recent study, it seems that women take advantage of the recovery of the labor market to achieve financial independence, which allows them to end unhappy marriages.[18]

In *The Moral Consequences of Economic Growth*, the economist Benjamin Friedman shows that there is a remarkable parallel between the phases of economic growth and the rise of "progressive" ideas.[19] Friedman analyzes the major waves of American and European political life in relation to the economic climate. The "progressive" periods of American life, whether 1865–1880, 1895–1919, or the civil rights era following World War II, almost always go hand in hand with strong growth. In France as well, growth periods—the Third Republic, the postwar era—were marked by intense reformist activity. By contrast, economic crises were accompanied by the rise of populist movements: Boulangism, Action Française, Fascist violence, Vichy, and the growth of the Front National all surfaced at a time of crisis. In Germany, the expansion of civil and social rights (German unity, Willy Brandt's reforms) took place during growth phases. The Nazis' rise in the thirties and fresh outbreaks of anti-immigrant impulses made their appearance during phases of severe recession.

KONDRATIEV'S SECOND DEMISE

Unfortunately, the new Kondratiev wave did not fulfill its promise. The pendulum swing came to an abrupt halt. By the early 2000s, even before the financial crisis, growth slowed. In 2008, with the bankruptcy of Lehmann Brothers, a huge shock wave reverberated across the world. All countries were struck at the same time. In 2009, industrial production and world trade fell by more than 10 percent. Such high figures had never been recorded earlier in so short a time, not even in the thirties. It would take ten years for the crisis to be resolved.

The financial crisis did not come out of the blue. It was the result of imbalances that had been piling up since the beginning of the conservative revolution. The major problem that the new Kondratiev wave had encountered was that, contrary to Reagan's declaration, wealth did not trickle down. The *World Inequality Report*, by Thomas Piketty and coauthors, sheds a stark light on the process in place over nearly forty years.[20] In the United States, the share of national income in the hands of the wealthiest 1 percent has doubled, from 10 percent to 20 percent of the total. What is extraordinary is that this increase in wealth has come about almost exclusively at the expense of the poorest 50 percent. Their share, in fact, fell from 20 percent to 10 percent of global income, in a huge shift in favor of the wealthiest. This also means that, whereas in 1980 the wealthiest earned twenty-five times more than the poorest, they now earn a hundred times more. During the last forty years, the poorest 50 percent have made no progress in their purchasing power. No trickle-down effect has been observed. When growth benefits only 10 percent of the population, it is clearly fragile. The poor must go into debt to hold onto their place in society. In the United States, the housing bubble encouraged them to take out mortgages on their property, resulting in an untenable pyramiding of debt. That bubble burst with the financial crisis of 2007–2008, prematurely interrupting the peak phase of the Kondratiev wave.

THE NEW SPIRIT OF CAPITALISM

Long before it was a technological revolution, the conservative revolution set in motion a financial one. Beginning in the eighties, shareholders took over the management of businesses, triggering a complete overhaul of industrial capitalism. The model for organizing work that prevailed after the war, with its social policy and trade unions, was called into question. Profit-sharing bonuses replaced career development. The organizational norms of the new "stockholder capitalism" reduced the activities of firms to the area of their expertise, their "core business." All the rest was left to the market. Outsourcing and subcontracting became the rule. The industrial model of the large corporation encompassing all social strata would be shattered.

While the unions pushed for an egalitarian wage structure, the new world separated the different segments of society from one another. A study by Richard Freeman and coauthors has shown that skyrocketing inequality in America can be entirely explained by the rise in inequality between firms rather than within them.[21] In a typical business of the fifties and sixties, food services, security, janitorial services, and accounting were done by salaried employees of the firm. With the increase in outsourcing, none of these services is performed internally any longer. External service providers no longer enjoy the status and pay scale of the business that hires them. The new system is moving in the direction of businesses without employees, a process made possible by the new information and communication technologies. With the arrival of globalization, increasing competition and cheaper labor completed this movement. But the chronology shows that the internal reorganization of capitalism preceded globalization.

It's as if the new technologies had above all allowed businesses to cut costs. As Philippe Askenazy shows, the first firms to be reorganized were those with the highest rate of unionization, proof that the target was really the old Fordist compromise between unions and management. "IT productivity" increases in a business only when it is accompanied by an overhaul of the previous work organization.[22] Data processing makes it possible to track idle time "scientifically." The manager who types her own texts, the bank employee who performs the tasks previously assigned to several people, and the night watchman at a hotel who does the accounting in the daytime are all examples of a world "without downtime." Gains in productivity were achieved, but they resulted from one primordial factor: the intensification of labor. It was during this period that "the cult of performance," to borrow the title of Alain Ehrenberg's book, became ingrained.[23] For Philippe Askenazy, a " neo-Stakhanovism" became the order of the day.

As Boltanski and Chiapello note, the "new spirit of capitalism" has often taken inspiration from the language invented in the sixties to theorize the challenge to the old Taylorist model.[24] In favoring multitasking, the capacity to learn and to adapt to new functions, New Managerialism has turned toward what is known as *savoir-être* (knowing how to be) rather than *savoir-faire* (know how, "knowing how to do"). However, as Askenazy points out in *Work Disturbances*, in reality the workers have become both more autonomous *and* more constrained.[25] They must keep pace with the client's or contractor's demand. The "just in time" culture, imported from Japan, makes "total customer satisfaction" the essential issue. "The arrival of a reactive productivism, which was heralded as an improvement, even a form of emancipation from the Taylorist model, was in reality accompanied by a deterioration in working conditions and an intensification of work." The increase in psychological disorders went hand in hand with physical problems (musculoskeletal disorders, for example). Stress itself was the result of a major contradictory injunction: "Do it well and quickly!"

Even as labor costs were being completely reevaluated, an enormous financial orgy was taking place. The stock market, defying gravity, increased tenfold between 1980 and 2000. President George W. Bush, who spoke from experience, summed it up in the expression: "Wall Street got drunk." In the midst of the crisis, the *Financial Times* cited a study calculating the remuneration of the directors of the largest financial institutions in the three years preceding the subprime mortgage crisis. They earned some $100 billion in income, later leaving $4 trillion of losses to the community. In a very short period of time, the managers, who had been salaried employees like everyone else, ceased to be so. In the old industrial world, they would never have dared increase their remuneration without ensuring that their subordinates benefited as well. In the general cost-cutting set in place, the opposite has occurred. Their destinies and their remuneration have come to be indexed to the stock market.

In Max Weber's classic work, *The Protestant Ethic and the Spirit of Capitalism*, the author argues that capitalism is not characterized by the desire for money. If that were the case, it would have developed in the Middle East, among Phoenician merchants, or in a Venice enriched by the spice trade. But it appeared in England, then developed in the United States and northern Europe. Although Weber acknowledges that greed constitutes one of the fundamental motivations of human activity, he argues that capitalism tends to rationalize that appetite, building contractual and trust-based relationships, reestablishing a new overall balance with rules, laws, and an "ethic" of responsibility. The restoration promised by the conservative revolution may have been understood as a return to the founding values of capitalism, those of the Puritans, but it ushered in the opposite: the triumph of greed.

PART II

A Time of Debasement

CHAPTER FOUR

The Proletariat's Farewell

AT A TIME when the unbridled capitalism launched by Reagan and Thatcher's conservative revolution was prevailing, the old specter of populism came back to haunt the West. It replaced communism, which had collapsed in 1989 when the unthinkable happened: the fall of the Berlin Wall. Communism, the secular religion of the industrial world, vanished. The philosopher Emmanuel Levinas writes that the fall of the wall, in eliminating "the horizon of a secular hope, shook to the core the categories of thought that sustained philosophical reflection. For even though the Soviet state had become the most terrible of all, it still bore a promise of deliverance, a hope of liberation. With the collapse of the Soviet system, our relationship to time entered a phase of crisis."[1] And in fact, the feeling that the world was meaningless would very quickly become pervasive in this new period.

The philosopher Peter Sloterdijk, commenting on the fall of the USSR, speaks of a "bank of rage" that abruptly went bankrupt.[2] Whom could the people turn to, he asks, when they find themselves filled with rage? The answer was not long in coming. It originated in the populist parties, which would burgeon subsequently. That "rage" was in part the result of the failure of the Left and then of the Right to support the aspirations of the working classes. The Left failed to protect them from the crisis, sometimes creating the impression they were accommodating themselves to it, and the Right, elected on a platform of moral restoration, sacrificed them on the altar of greed. The working classes were hard-hit by the dissolution of industrial society, which despite its flaws had at least had the advantage of creating an inclusive social environment. The sociologist Max Schuler has elaborated a theory of resentment, of which populism is the perfect expression.[3] He allows to analyze populism as a specifically modern phenomenon, intrinsic to the societies where formal social equality among individuals coexists with spectacular differences in power, education, status, and property, differences that are suddenly intolerable when it becomes clear they are irreducible.

The term "populism" must be used with caution. In some circles, it is confused with "popular" and simply expresses the contempt of the elites for the masses. It has an august history, however. In Russia between 1840 and 1880, the populist (Narodnik) movement was animated by teachers, civil servants, and journalists. They launched a drive for popular education, one of whose repercussions would be the 1917 Russian Revolution. In the United States, populism surfaced in the 1880s in the world of small farmers of the South and the West. The farmers, overburdened with debt, turned against their bankers, giving rise to a true agrarian insurrection from the 1870s through the 1890s. The People's Party managed to elect a few senators and would demand the nationalization of the railroads, telegraph companies, national resources, and banks. Debt forgiveness was at the center of these demands. A biblical dimension was sometimes added: The jubilee, according to the Bible, prescribes that debts be forgiven every fifty years.

Latin America was for a long time the testing ground for populism. Moreover some would say that it is the only continent where the term really has any meaning. Argentine Peronism is its exemplary figure, but it is not an isolated one. Populism similarly left its mark in Brazil, Chile, Colombia, Peru, and Venezuela. In an enlightening book published in 1990, Rudiger Dornbusch and Sebastian Edwards define populism's economic program as the pursuit of inclusive growth with an absolute contempt for the macroeconomic objectives of stability.[4] The same cycle recurs endlessly in Latin America, like a neurosis. Each time, an ill-conceived fiscal stimulus leads to a deterioration in the balance of payments, a fall in the exchange rate, runaway inflation, and the collapse of production. "All these policies occur in profoundly inegalitarian societies, an inequality that, curiously, the policies never manage to solve."

Dominique Reynié, characterizing the European populism of France's Le Pen, Hungary's Victor Orbán, and the coalition in Italy between the League and the Five Star Movement, speaks of a "patrimonialist populism."[5] It promises voters a welfare state "for them," cities "for them," work "for them." It has combined a dual hatred: of the elites above *and* the immigrants below, both of whom are supposedly responsible for social unrest. Granted, there is a radicalism on the Left that checks the first box—hatred of the elites—but its electoral results are poorer than that of the Right, because it lacks the second, essential item: xenophobia.

The Sweden Democrats, the Danish People's Party, the Finns Party, the Freedom Party of Austria, the Golden Dawn in Greece, and the League in Italy were all built on xenophobia. The founder of the Five Star Movement, Beppe Grillo (ineligible to hold office because he was convicted of involuntary manslaughter after a car accident in 1981), also struck up the nationalist tune, though the movement itself is more vague in this respect. He accused immigrants of being responsible for the return to Italy of tuberculosis. Here is how Grillo recommends dealing with an immigrant, quoting Reynié: "You take him, you load him into a car without anyone seeing you, you take him to a corner, and you give him two good slaps." And Grillo adds: "Thank me for being here, otherwise, you would have the neo-Nazis." "That assertion is more threatening then reassuring," concludes Reynié.

The French National Front is emblematic of that new populism. It has sought to harness popular discontent, but only as it were in fits and starts. Originally economically liberal, the Le Pen family jumped on the bandwagon of the other iterations of European populism, criticizing both the elites and immigrants. The party was created in 1972. In 1974 Jean-Marie Le Pen received 0.75 percent of the vote in the presidential election. In 1981 he did not manage to collect enough signatures to qualify as a candidate. But in 1984, to everyone's surprise, he received 11 percent of the vote in the European Union elections. The party initially drew inspiration from Reagan, criticizing the Left in power, especially on the "anti-tax" issue. In 1988 Le Pen received 14.4 percent of the votes cast, and in 2002 he reached the second round of the presidential election. But this victory was deceptive. The call for lower taxes and the anti-immigrant sentiments formed a cocktail that the classic Right could easily make their own. Sarkozy's candidacy in 2007 relegated Jean-Marie Le Pen to 10.4 percent of the vote, stopping him in his tracks.

The party's rebirth came from his daughter Marine. She proposed an "ethno-socialism," in Reynié's expression, which stunned the Left and the Right. More radical than the Left economically, more radical than the Right in the realm of values, she appealed to large contingents of the working classes who believe they have been left behind by globalization and are the hardest hit by immigration. Her personal career path was finally cut short by a completely botched performance against Emmanuel Macron in the 2017 presidential election, in which, however she ranked much higher in the second round than had her father.

2016, Annus Horribilis

2016 remains to this day the apotheosis of that growing exasperation. It marked the entry of populism into the "reality" of political life, with Brexit and the election of Donald Trump. The polls taken by the Lord Ashcroft Institute after the Brexit vote leave no doubt about the feelings of those who voted to leave the European Union: They hate the words *feminism*, *multiculturalism*, and *ecology*, but also *capitalism* and *Internet*. *The Economist*, newspaper of the British establishment, chose as an example the city where the "Yes" vote for Brexit was highest: Boston, a small town in Lincolnshire (not to be confused with the American city, home of MIT and Harvard), where 76 percent of voters chose to leave the European Union. Seventy percent of the population left school at the age of sixteen. The quays of the port are empty. Cafés and new shops have names like Polski-Sklep and U Ani. Thirteen percent of Boston's residents are immigrants: Most are Poles and Lithuanians who work on small neighboring farms. "It was time we took back control," said a retiree. The city was lulled into nostalgia for its past greatness, when it was one of the hubs of trade with the Netherlands. A majestic church continues to dominate the still-elegant city center. Boston is a reflection of the 52 percent of British citizens who voted against the European Union. It is at war with the 48 percent who voted to remain: the young, the educated, and the liberal, who live in

London, Bristol, Manchester, or Cambridge, the most dynamic urban centers.

The second boisterous act in populism's rise to power was the election of Donald Trump in November 2016. The same resentment was being expressed, that of "Whites without a college education," those who live in what urban elites call the "flyover states" between New York and Los Angeles. Two-thirds of Whites without a college education voted for Trump.[6] When asked, "Do you think the next generation will be in better shape than we are today?" those who answered "No" voted for Trump at a rate of 63 percent. Of the optimists, 59 percent chose Hillary Clinton. Here we find the suffering of those who live in rural environments and loathe the values of the big cities.[7] What does Trump offer them? Only this: an acknowledgment of their suffering, of their difficulty holding onto a place in a world that is driving them out.

In 2004 the writer Thomas Frank published a work which asks the key question: Why do the poor vote on the right?[8] Kansas, his home state, provided him with a great test case to search for an answer. In rural towns, he wrote, we are witnessing "a civilization in the early stages of irreversible decline." One of these towns sold its public school on eBay. For a long time, Wichita, "The Air Capital of the World," was a strongly unionized working-class city and one of the strongholds of local Democrats. The city was for Boeing what Detroit was for Ford and General Motors. It was hard-hit by the crisis of the 2000s, when Boeing's payroll was cut in half. In the nineties Wichita had become one of the chief Republican bastions in Kansas, a powerful fortress where the wars against abortion and Darwin's theories are waged.

Republicans before Trump had settled into a combination of moral conservatism and economic liberalism. Their election campaigns promised to ban abortion and gay rights, which had no material effects but would implement a concrete program of ultra-liberal economic liberalization. In reality, the Tea Party movement within the Republican Party pushed through a program of tax cuts that aggravated the economic problem and the social crisis, thus setting up a second round of moral protest.

During the primaries, Trump took a different tack. He did not concern himself with the Tea Party's obsessions, especially on the subject of abortion, and he attacked the Republican establishment on another front, the openness of borders to immigrants and goods. Going against the party's orthodoxy, he denounced free trade agreements with Mexico and China, and focused on the fight against immigration, promising to build a wall along the Mexican border—as in the series "Game of Thrones"—and to hunt down those who are in the country illegally. Xenophobia and protectionism were his chief watchwords, hammered in without restraint.

Rhetorically speaking, Trump's language is characterized by personal attacks on his opponents. Journalists who criticize him are accused of being sellouts to the powers that be, of being part of the establishment. In lambasting "political correctness," Trump sends the message that he is unlike everyone else, that he is "authentic." The more out of control he gets, the more he demonstrates his sincerity. As economists who specialize in the media know, he has to lay it on thick to show he is different. In piling on the misogynous and xenophobic remarks, he indicates he is a fan of plain speaking. But in actuality his voters understand perfectly well that he really is racist and misogynistic. His criticism of political correctness is the mask that allows him to say openly what he really thinks.

Trump has called Mexicans "rapists." He defends torture and believes that nuclear war ought to be a tactical option. He made fun of a reporter with a disability and intimated that a woman reporter he found too aggressive was on her period. He was caught on video boasting about grabbing women by the genitals. Stephen Bannon, who was his henchman for a time before they had a falling-out, ran the Far-Right Web site Breitbart News, which attracts those who believe in white supremacy, oppose immigration, feminism, and multiculturalism, and get a kick out of incessant attacks on Jews, Muslims, and other groups that it finds unworthy.

Many commentators, especially in Europe, interpreted Trump's election as the end of the liberal economic cycle that began with Reagan, a call to ease market pressure, a needed corrective to the staggering increase in inequality. When the list of the members of his first cabinet was made public, however, it quickly became clear that Trump's election did not mark the end of economic liberalism. As secretary of state he appointed Rex Tillerson, president of the oil giant Exxon, a strong advocate of the liberalization of the energy market and a good friend of Putin. Steven Mnuchin, named secretary of the treasury, is a former partner at Goldman Sachs and a Hollywood financier who got rich buying up property titles from households bankrupted by the subprime mortgage crisis. The nominee for labor secretary was Andrew Puzder, former chief executive officer of CKE, a chain of fast-food restaurants, who declared himself opposed to any increase in the minimum wage. He had to withdraw his name, however, because he had employed an undocumented immigrant housekeeper. Also among Trump's advisers was Carl Icahn, formerly a corporate raider who served as the model for Gekko, a character in Oliver Stone's *Wall Street* and inspired the slogan "Greed is good!"

Trump thus formed a (first) government made up of billionaires like himself, worth more than $6 billion according to *The Economist*. None of the secretaries originally appointed remained in office for very long, however. What characterizes Trump above all is a desire to abolish the rules, even at the highest echelons of the state. Through all the shakeups in his administrative staff, Trump has shown that his principal orientation is hatred of international rules: the Paris climate accord, the regulations of the WTO and of NATO.

Trump's election can be interpreted as a manifestation of the power of the Freudian id, of "fuck the rules" and of "It's no use." With these subliminal slogans, which could have been those of May '68, Trump attracted the votes of the American working classes, by denouncing the politically correct, those who want to ban carrying arms, to force people to respect environmental standards, to stop smoking. In *Nothing More to Be Done, Nothing More to Give a Damn About!* Brice Teinturier has analyzed the phenomenon of "fed-up" French voters in the same terms, as a general crisis of confidence in democracy itself. [9]

Michael Sandel, a professor of philosophy at Harvard University and the author of a best-seller titled *Justice*, goes even further.[10] In his view, the enemy of the working classes is in reality the superego of the leftist elites, who argue for universal access to school, health care, and the promise of social ascent. These elites have not understood that, to the ears of those who did not pursue higher education, do not eat organic, and do not have a healthy lifestyle, this meritocratic ideal sounded like an accusation, a reproach. The working classes interpreted these measures as the arrogance of elites advocating the advent of a world created in their image. The vote for Trump was the manifestation of a frantic need for acknowledgment, social esteem. His voters want to be loved for what they are and not for what they could have or should have been.

History Goes in Circles

A fear of the future and the xenophobic, nihilistic passions that accompany it are nothing new. They are characteristic of periods of doubt, when a society loses confidence in itself.

Nothing is more enlightening in that respect than an analysis of the shift that occurred between the twenties and the thirties, beginning in the United States.

The twenties were called the *Roaring Twenties*, ten glorious years of American growth. Electric lighting, running water, and elevators completely changed the conditions of urban existence. The American way of life led consumers to discover the delights of buying (on credit) a wide range of new products: automobiles, radios, household appliances. The decade was also an intense period in the nation's cultural life. Sinclair Lewis, F. Scott Fitzgerald, and Ernest Hemingway brought about a revival in American literature. The first talkie, *The Jazz Singer*, came to theaters in 1928.

During that golden decade, the moral codes of American society were revamped by enthusiastic young people, just as they would be fifty years later, in the sixties. Women cut their hair short and dressed as boys. Images spread of sexually liberated woman, or "flappers." Fitzgerald writes of them in his *Flappers and Philosophers*, short stories published in 1920, the year American women earned the right to vote. A growing number of women joined the labor market, earning their financial independence for the first time.

The 1920s saw the emergence everywhere of an avant-garde in revolt. Ian Kershaw notes the rise of opposition to "previous forms of representation, which they regarded as outmoded, superficial, devoid of inner meaning."[11] Modern art, inspired by psychoanalysis, wanted to show the absurd, inexplicable chaos of the passions. Paris was the center of that vitality. Pablo Picasso, James Joyce, and Ezra Pound ended up there. In Germany, art and social thought also espoused that new spirit of the time. The Bauhaus, founded by Walter Gropius in 1919, brought together artists, sculptors, and architects, in an "extraordinary efflorescence of avant-garde cultural and intellectual creativity."

Already, however, a cultural backlash was in the works. The prohibition of alcohol, passed in 1919, was one of its emblematic measures. That backlash would fully deploy with the Great Depression, which began in 1929. The frivolity and sensuality of the twenties vanished as quickly as they had appeared. Women lengthened their skirts, began to wear gloves. People became less exuberant, and tolerance toward deviant attitudes fell. Kershaw sums up the period as follows: "The economic crisis greatly sharpened already existing sources of anger and resentment. It made societies meaner, less tolerant. One indicator . . . was the increased prejudice against women in work holding 'men's jobs.'" In his anti-Semitic broadcasts, the radio priest Father Coughlin reached millions of listeners. Philip Roth, in a merciless and ironic book titled *The Plot against America* (2004), constructs a perfectly credible narrative about an America that chose to elect not Franklin Roosevelt but Charles Lindberg, the first pilot to cross the Atlantic (in 1927), a national hero and notorious anti-Semite.

In Europe, American culture became the symbol of the moral failings of modernity. Jazz was called *nigger music*, believed inferior to the advances in civilization represented by Bach and Beethoven. The erotic rhythms of "American" dance were lambasted for threatening the morals of young ladies. Culture gone amuck seemed to be personified in the naked body of Josephine Baker, an African American singer and dancer who took Paris and Berlin by storm, dressed in little more than a skirt of rubber bananas.

With the crisis, the idea of getting rid of "defectives" by means of "racial hygiene" gained ground everywhere. As early as 1932, voluntary sterilization programs were introduced in Germany for people suffering from hereditary diseases. But eugenics was by no means peculiar to that country. The Eugenics Society was created in Great Britain in 1926. Described as a form of social Darwinism, eugenics was an English theory developed by Charles Darwin's cousin Francis Galton, who found supporters among thinkers reputed to be iconoclasts: John Maynard Keynes, William Henry Beveridge, H. G. Wells, George Bernard Shaw.[12] In Sweden, an institute for racial biology was established in Uppsala in 1922.

THE SOURCES OF TOTALITARIANISM

Until the war, however, the overwhelming majority of the populations in Great Britain, France, and the United States would continue to support the democratic system in place. Despite the pressure exerted by moral conservatism, Roosevelt reinvented the Democratic Left, no doubt because his predecessor, Herbert Hoover, who had presided over the economic disaster, was on the other side. Democracy was first breached in Germany, when the old wounds of the war broke open once again. Oswald Spengler's *Decline of the West* would play a major role in the drama of German pessimism: The first volume was published in 1918, just before the end of the war, the second four years later. As in the riddle of the Sphinx, civilizations, according to Spengler, go through three stages, childhood, adulthood, and old age, at which point the vital force of a society is totally drained, and the society must change.

In her masterpiece *The Origins of Totalitarianism*, Hannah Arendt dove headlong into the moral collapse of the thirties, providing a remarkable reservoir of concepts for understanding the current rise of populism.[13] According to Arendt, totalitarianism can be interpreted as the emotional response of isolated individuals united by hatred of the established order in the face of an atomized society. Bankrupt small landowners, the middle classes who lost their standing because of the crisis— in short, all those who had believed they had found a place in society and then lost it—formed the battalions of resentment. "In this atmosphere of the breakdown of class society the psychology of the European mass man developed. The fact that with monotonous but also abstract uniformity the same fate had befallen a mass of individuals did not prevent their judging themselves in terms of individual failure or the world in terms of specific injustice."

Among the authors Arendt invokes to grasp the debasement of the time was Gustave Le Bon, who in *Group Psychology and the Analysis of the Ego* analyzed how the individual's rationality can disintegrate when subjected to the emotional impulses of the mob. Arendt defined the generation to which she belonged as the one that witnessed, socially, "the transformation of a class system into a mass society; and spiritually, it was the rise of nihilism, which had long been the concern of a few but which suddenly become a mass phenomenon."[14]

Arendt adds that the masses, unlike social classes, are not united by a consciousness of a common interest. They do not have the specific mindset that finds expression in the pursuit of precise, limited, and accessible objectives. "The term masses applies only where we deal with people who . . . cannot be integrated into any organization based on common interest, into political parties or municipal governments or professional organizations or trade unions. . . . It was characteristic of the rise of the Nazi movement in Germany . . . [that it] recruited members from this mass of apparently indifferent people whom all other parties had given up." The *Volksgemeinschaft* promised absolute equality to all Germans, an equality not of laws but of nature. This allowed them to elevate themselves above the promise of a classless society, which threatened to pull everyone down.

The masses, Arendt concludes, are obsessed with the desire to escape reality because, essentially rootless, they can not longer bear its accidental and incomprehensible aspects. Nazi propaganda was characterized by a complete contempt for the facts: In the Nazis' view, the masses were entirely dependent on the power of the one who had created them. When Hitler decided to murder the insane, to get rid of unnecessary mouths to feed, he claimed, this was not really an economic calculation: "He was preparing the masses to abandon morality, to undertake a campaign of murders."

With the defeat of Nazism, the fictitious world it had created collapsed as quickly as it had come. The masses returned to their former status, that of isolated individuals, some of them happy to accept a function in the new world, others falling back into their former superfluity and desperation. After the war, the Allies tried in vain to find one committed Nazi among the German people, even though 90 percent of them had probably been sincere sympathizers at one time or another.

Fifty Years of Solitude

(LOST ILLUSIONS 3/3)

Clearly, no comparison is possible between the thirties and the current rise of populism. Our society has become more civilized. But the deterioration of contemporary political life is starkly reminiscent of Arendt's description of the rise of totalitarianism. The loss of the working classes' landmarks and the sense that class society, in which everyone had a place, has been destroyed, leaving people lost in an unstructured mass, are fundamental elements that shed light on the causes of the rise of contemporary populism.

An analysis of voting patterns in the French presidential election of 2017 gives a glimpse of the nature of that parallel. Votes for Le Pen increased in proportion to the distance separating voters from a major metropolitan area. Being relegated to places of residence far from the city centers contributes to their social isolation. An econometric analysis of the factors that determined the vote for the French presidential election of 2017, conducted on the basis of a survey by the Centre de recherches politiques de Sciences Po (Paris Institute of Political Studies), shows that the individual characteristics of Le Pen's voters carry a great deal more weight than their social background.[15] The profession of a voter's father, for example, statistically predicts which other candidates he or she will vote for, but it has no predictive value as to votes for Marine Le Pen.[16] Likewise, the average income in the district of residence is in general an explanatory factor (predicting a vote for the Left if income is low, for the Right if it is high), but not in the case of Le Pen. It is the voter's personal situation, individual income level, and subjective dissatisfaction that account for a vote for the National Front.[17]

In his characterization of our era, the sociologist Robert Castel has distinguished between the "positive individualism" of those whose social lives are successful and who can believe they are emancipated from social conventions, and "negative individualism," that which afflicts the working classes who lose confidence in themselves.[18] This distinction sheds light on the new political polarization. The opposition between Marine Le Pen voters and Macron voters can be graphed as a perfect diagonal, between those who have nothing—neither education nor income—and those who have everything, including subjective well-being. This diagonal is very different from the one that graphs the distinction between the Left and the Right, which marks an opposition not between the rich and the poor but between some rich and some poor. Still according to the CEVIPOF survey, Mélenchon voters have less money than Fillon voters, but on average their level of education is the same. They are frustrated by a social inequality they consider unjust and that they want to correct. Le Pen voters are like Trump voters: "Whites without a college education." They have lost all confidence in the meritocratic values of society. Their skepticism is so great that they no longer believe that the state can help them. They have very little interest in tax redistribution measures, even though their income level would make them the principal beneficiaries. Their paradoxical demand is "protection without redistribution," which explains why they call for the construction of walls against the rest of the world.

Le Pen voters have no class consciousness in the sense that was given to that term to explain the Communist vote. According to Hervé Le Bras, there is no correlation between the geography of the former Communist vote and that of the National Front vote at present.[19] The working class that expressed its approval for Le Pen is different from the working class that once voted for the Communist Party. In *Equality of Opportunity* (2002), the economist and sociologist Éric Maurin offers an analysis of the condition of workers that sheds light on that transformation. Alongside "industrial-type" workers, a growing share of artisanal-type workers must be counted, plus another category, those assigned to logistics (drivers, warehouse workers, and so on). These new groups are increasingly immersed in informal contexts, closer to the customer and to final demand than the industrial proletariat, who worked on the assembly lines and the factory floors of very large, heavy industry factories. Workers of the artisanal type work for smaller companies or as services providers for large firms. They typically work in construction, food services, or maintenance and repair. Those in the last category, drivers and warehouse workers, are akin to service providers: Their skills are much more individualized than the others. Whereas the industrial sector has lost more than a third of its workforce, the other sectors have stood up much better. Those in logistics and transportation have even made headway. In the postindustrial service sector, it is that "new working class" that is coming to the fore. "Delivery drivers or domestic workers are much more autonomous," Maurin explains, "They are involved in their work in a more direct and personal way than workers on the automobile assembly line." In artisanal-type environments, employees of small companies often espouse the ideology of their employer. They curse expenses, the dictatorship of the customer, and standards, all of which impose constraints on business operations and, according to them, ultimately keep wages low.

Émile Durkheim's analysis of suicide provides an enlightening parallel by which to understand the populist vote. For Durkheim, one of the founders of French sociology, the loss of sociability is one of the explanatory variables for suicide, which leads Durkheim to claim that suicide is a social and not an individual phenomenon. As Hervé Le Bras notes, there is no statistical correlation between the phenomena but rather a "parallelism" of the two situations, a loneliness that has become unbearable. The National Front vote is the expression of the malaise that results from the destruction not only of the industrial world but of the sociability of entire regions. One of the lessons of Le Bras's analysis, which is based on the studies of social geography he conducted with Emmanuel Todd, is that the regions that best withstand the encroachment of the National Front are those where family structures are the most solid. In the southwest of France, where the "extended family" has long been predominant, the National Front has not made inroads. Conversely, in the northeast, which has a tradition of nuclear, individualistic families, the isolation becomes overwhelming. The National Front is much stronger there.

Durkheim himself had in mind the moral crisis created by the rural exodus. The "anonymous" city was interpreted as one of the causes of suicide. Before him, Auguste Comte and Frédéric Le Play had already criticized the individualism of their time, emphasizing how harmful it was to social cohesion. It seems that the same diagnosis, with certain adaptations, can be made now. The sociologist Serge Paugam, for example, has analyzed today's social disconnectedness, in a book whose title aptly sums up his thesis: *Living Together in an Uncertain World*.[20] "Individuals are not truly themselves, do not fully achieve their potential, unless they form attachments [to society]. A [social] bond is strong when it allows individuals to ensure their protection against the vicissitudes of life and to satisfy their vital need for acknowledgment, the source of their identity and existence as human beings." Such is the great social question today.

Economic insecurity is the principal cause of social disconnection. "The development of wage insecurity constitutes one of the essential factors in the social integration crisis." But what has produced an additional shock wave during the crisis is that all other social bonds—family or friends—amplify in their own way rising inequalities. In a study he conducted in the Paris urban area, Paugam calculated that 20 percent of workers' children had practically no relationship with their (still-living) father or mother, compared to 5 percent of executives' children. It is as if economic and cultural inequalities are exacerbated by "elective" inequalities: the rate of participation in community organizations in wealthy neighborhoods, for example, is twice that of working-class neighborhoods, even within the Paris metropolitan area.[21]

Already in *Anti-Oedipus*, a milestone when it was published in 1972, Gilles Deleuze and Félix Guattari had focused on the problem of social disconnection.[22] Capitalism, they explain, constantly calls into question the bonds of ordinary life. In precapitalist societies, strict rules govern all circumstances of life, whereas capitalism continually abolishes these rules. It "deterritorializes" individuals. Peasants leave their lands, workers their factories. Human beings lose their particularities, their qualities, becoming labor and nothing more. Capitalism thus creates a world of anxieties that must be treated subsequently. It is necessary, in order to heal these anxieties, to build "artificial territorialities"—states, nations, families—to replace those capitalism has destroyed.

As a result, Deleuze and Guattari explain, in the florid language of post–May '68, individuals have two options. The first is to obey the social rules of the herd, whether it's a question of the nation or money. Desire is vested in authorities, institutions, honors: "Values, morals, nations, religions, and the private beliefs that our vanity and complaisance generously grant us, [which] are deceptive dwellings that the world furnishes to those who think they can thereby remain standing and at rest, among stable things." The other path open to individuals is to successfully break through, to "cross the line" that separates normal people from the artist's "desiring-production." It is a very tricky transition, which can lead individuals who fail "to slip into a state of depression and resentment." What Deleuze and Guattari had not foreseen, but which their analysis allows us to understand, is the tremendous division of the social world that the disintegration of the industrial world would produce, rather than the evolution of society as a whole. A new "deterritorialization" has occurred. It has granted the condition of artist to the winners and resentment to the losers.

CHAPTER FIVE

Immigration Phobia

IN AN ENIGMATIC SENTENCE like others for which he had a flair, the psychoanalyst Jacques Lacan announced the return of racism in the seventies with the following explanation: "Only the Other situates our *jouissance* in its waywardness, but does so insofar as we are separated from the Other."[1] Against all odds—given the moment when it was made—this remark by Lacan has proved prophetic. Granted, outbreaks of xenophobia have flared up repeatedly in history, reaching a first peak in the twenties and thirties. In the United States at that time, they were directed primarily against populations from Asia. This is, however, the first time since the end of World War II that they have attained such a fever pitch in the Western countries. Before Trump, neither Reagan nor either Bush had succumbed to xenophobia.

The striking thing at present is the universality of the phenomenon. Far-Right parties with a strong xenophobic coloration have surged up everywhere, even in the Scandinavian countries, despite the fact that they are better protected from rising inequities. As Lacan suggested, the new xenophobia truly seems to be part of a general phobia directed at the other, whoever that might be. As the French CEVIPOF survey shows, National Front voters display a widespread distrust of others, whether strangers in the street, neighbors on the same floor of their apartment building, co-workers, or even members of their own family.[2]

It is Mexicans who have been the object of Trump's xenophobic phobias and those of his voters. In Great Britain, the Poles have been targeted by the pro-Brexit campaign. The argument often used in France, in which Islam is presented as the problem, thus doesn't work for understanding the nature of the phenomenon. Throughout Europe, the Muslim population is small (Muslims comprise only 3.6 percent of the total population). In this area as in many others, there is a considerable difference between perception and reality: Polls reveal that the perceived number of immigrants is nearly triple the actual number.

But what about the "real" economic issues relating to the phenomenon of immigration? What are its effects on the condition of the working classes in the host country? The first paradox is that, though everyone these days is talking about immigration, it is now half to one-third the levels of the last century, relative to the global population. During the vast immigration movement between 1870 and 1910, Argentina, for example, saw an increase in its labor force of more than 75 percent. In Canada and Australia, the increase was about 40 percent; in the United States, 21 percent. Of the countries with net emigration, Sweden lost 40 percent of its adult population, Italy nearly 30 percent. In the nineteenth century, an Italian or Swede earned one-quarter that earned by an American. At present, a Salvadoran living in the United States earns seven times that of a worker living in El Salvador.[3] Migration is much lower, even though the benefits are much greater. It is the cost of migrating that has changed in nature: What has increased is not transportation costs but the price of crossing the border.

What are the merits of the economic arguments for and against immigration? The economist Lant Pritchett provides a superb argument in its favor.[4] He cites an old, fairly radical estimate from Bob Hamilton and George Whalley: They calculated that the global GDP could double if all restrictions on human mobility were abolished. A more recent and less ambitious model from the World Bank estimated that a 3 percent increase in immigration would yield five times more revenues than the abolition of (remaining) restrictions on international trade. What is the impact of immigration on resident populations? Economists are sharply divided on this point. According to David Card, a professor at the University of California Berkeley, immigrants create jobs over and above those already existing, without affecting the condition of workers in the host countries.[5] He takes as an example the sudden arrival of 125,000 Cuban immigrants in Miami in 1980, representing 7 percent of the local active population, which had no negative impact on the city's residents.

Card's article has been criticized by another famous economist, George Borjas, a professor at Harvard and himself a Cuban immigrant. According to Borjas, an influx of immigrants does lower the wages of the native population.[6] He claims that Card did not adequately take into account the jobs actually affected by the Mariel boatlift.[7] Who are we to believe? Most economists side with Card, but only after making the following argument: Yes, the arrival of immigrants can lower pay for the jobs they do; but no, that does not affect the native populations because they leave these jobs to take others that are better paid. Historically, immigration for a long time allowed workers in the host country to move up a rung on the social ladder. Gérard Noiriel, analyzing employment in the Longwy mines, noted that 100 percent of underground workers were immigrants, as were 50 percent of those responsible for overseeing and transporting the ore, but that no immigrants—0 percent—worked in the offices. At present as well, the least "appealing" jobs—restaurant work, security, retail trade, elderly care—go to immigrants. They have been called *shit jobs*, which the native populations do not want, which first-generation immigrants do everywhere, and which the second generation would like to escape.

The essential point of the controversy is this: According to Borjas himself, the (potential) victims of international migration flows are native-born Blacks and Latinos. It is doubtful that these are the people Trump and Brexit are seeking to protect. In attacking immigrants, populists mask the real object of their phobia: It is the domestic poor who obsess them. Where they go wrong is in holding up a mirror in which they could recognize themselves, that of a society that has lost its cohesion. Immigration is much more than an economic issue. As René Girard would have said, immigrants are scapegoats of a society in crisis and have become a veritable fixation, the designated target of violence at the present time.[8]

Ultimi Barbarorum

"I heard Theo van Gogh beg for mercy. 'Don't do it! Don't do it!' he cried. I saw him fall onto the bicycle path. His killer was so calm. That really shocked me. How you can murder a person in such cold blood, right there in the street?" What most struck witnesses about Mohammed Bouyeri, a twenty-six-year old Moroccan Dutch, was his coldness. Videos of other murders were found in his apartment, including that of the American journalist Daniel Pearl. This quotation appears at the beginning of Ian Buruma's *Murder in Amsterdam*,[9] a companion piece, thirty years later, to Leonardo Sciascia's book on the murder of Aldo Moro. The leftist violence of the seventies and that of the jihadists of the 2000s mirror each other. But each is also a reflection of its time.

Theo van Gogh, the great-great-nephew of the painter Vincent van Gogh, was fascinated by Céline and the Marquis de Sade. His favorite film was Stanley Kubrick's *A Clockwork Orange*, about a gang of ultraviolent young people who howled unspeakable obscenities. In his first public skirmish, he accused the president of the Jewish community, Leon de Winter, himself the son of Orthodox Jews, of getting rich off the Holocaust. "Yellow stars copulating in the gas chambers," van Gogh also wrote. He then accused Job Cohen, the mayor of Amsterdam, of acting like a Nazi. In his relentless pursuit of provocation, van Gogh produced a documentary titled *Submission*, which projects quotations from the Qur'an onto the naked bodies of several veiled women. It is this film that triggered the violence of the Muslim community.

Van Gogh had himself fallen under the spell of Pim Fortuyn, the politician who reinvented the Dutch Far Right. Fortuyn invented a political tactic that had a considerable impact in Europe: the denunciation of Islam in the name of tolerance. In February 2002, responding to a question about his hostility toward Islam, he declared: "I have no desire . . . to have to go through the emancipation of women and homosexuals all over again. . . . They're a bit like those old Calvinists." Fortuyn emphasized that he and millions of others had worked hard to free themselves from the shackles of their own religion. "And here were these newcomers injecting society with religion once again."

Originally a professor of philosophy, a former Marxist who proudly proclaimed his homosexuality, Fortuyn liked to make a spectacle of himself. "Fortuyn's genius was theatrics. . . . The transformation from a mediocre academic into a popular cult figure was his final masterpiece." His book, *Autobiography of a Baby Boomer*, was a best seller. He spoke openly of his sexual adventures in saunas and back rooms. Fortuyn played up Islamophobia, even while boasting that he had had sex with Moroccan boys. His manner of justifying intolerance in the name of tolerance quickly inspired the other Far-Right European parties, the National Front in particular. He dressed up the ordinary xenophobia of these parties in new clothes.

Fortuyn too was murdered. His killer was a fanatical animal rights activist, Volker van der Graaf. As Buruma notes ironically, the fact that van Gogh's and Fortuyn's murderers both came on bicycles adds a "peculiarly Dutch flavor" to their crimes. Fortuyn's funeral has been compared to that of Diana, princess of Wales: Like her, explains Buruma, "He was a master of emotional kitsch." In November 2004, a poll to decide the most important Dutch personality placed Pim Fortuyn at the top, far ahead of William of Orange, Rembrandt, and Erasmus, not to mention Spinoza, who did not even make the list.

How did Fortuyn reach the top of the popularity polls, in a country known for its penchant for consensus and compromise? In the Netherlands, conflicts are usually settled through negotiation. In the eighties, while the rest of the world was being cast in the mold of Reaganism, the Dutch "polder model" was vaunted as an example of successful dialogue and cooperation. The "Wassenaar Arrangement," as it was known, established a pact in 1982 between trade unions and management that allowed the Netherlands to return to the path of growth more quickly than the other European countries.

The Netherlands—Amsterdam in particular—has a long history of welcoming foreigners. Sephardic Jews arrived in the Dutch Republic in the late sixteenth and early seventeenth centuries. A huge synagogue was built between 1671 and 1675.

The French Huguenots also sought refuge there, after Louis XIV revoked the Edict of Nantes in 1685. As Buruma points out, "It is surely no coincidence, if what is called the early Enlightenment of the Dutch Republic was partly inspired by the ideas of a son of Sephardic refugees in Amsterdam, Benedictus (Baruch) Spinoza." The brothers Johan and Cornelis de Witt, who had a passion for culture, were his patrons. Johan was prime minister (grand pensionary) from 1653 to 1672, the country's golden age. A mathematician in his spare time, he was also the author of a geometry book.

It is deeply troubling that it was the Netherlands, a country famous for its humanistic tradition, that reinvented the ideology of the Far Right. But every country has its dark side, and the Netherlands is no exception. There is another aspect to the national myth. The de Witt brothers, humanistic heroes of the country's golden age, were both murdered in The Hague in 1672, by a frenzied mob manipulated by the monarchists. Their death shattered Spinoza. He tried to plaster a tract called *Ultimi Barbarorum* (*The Last Barbarians*), on the city's walls, but was dissuaded by his lodger, who feared for Spinoza's life. This is one of the rare times when the author of the *Ethics* is known to have lost control of his emotions.

Fortuyn was the new face of that old Holland, the one that despised the elites, the *regenten* (regents) as they were called in the seventeenth century. This is not a new phenomenon coming out of nowhere with the crisis, but the expression of a tenacious hatred. The psychologist Shalom Schwartz perfectly illuminates the mechanisms of that resurgence.[10] In a study covering a large number of countries, he shows that the distribution of types of affect is astonishingly stable over time and across space ". To simplify, everywhere and always a quarter of the population will be idealists, a quarter opportunists, a quarter hedonists, and a quarter fascists. In his view, it is not human passions that change but the circumstances that give them the occasion to find expression.[11]

The affects can be reduced to four categories, but there is a much larger number of ways of combining them. Fortuyn, who went from the Far Left to the Far Right, synthesized two types of protests: against the system in general and against immigrants in particular.[12] Similarly, May '68 forged an alliance between the idealists and the hedonists, and collaborators in World War II sealed an accord between the fascists and the opportunists. As for the current immigration phobia, one can say that the crisis does not make racists of people who were not so beforehand: It creates the circumstances that allow racism to find expression without shame, by allying itself with other protests that make it more generally acceptable.

Postmodern Violence

The Far-Right parties blame immigrants for being "different." René Girard explains that, just as we find beautiful those we love because we love them and not because they are beautiful, racists need to create differences to understand what they themselves are by designating what they are not.[13] The cruel paradox is that immigrants usually do everything they can to integrate into the society where they have settled.

Ayaan Hirsi Ali, the young Somali-Dutch politician with whom van Gogh made the film *Submission*, splendidly illustrates this challenge. She managed to break free from her environment only after a long journey. Ian Buruma portrays her strikingly. When she was young, mere contact with her boyfriend's hand plunged her into a frightening state of anxiety and guilt. It was a revelation to her that young people could kiss each other on the mouth without feeling shame. One forgets, adds Buruma, the speed at which our own sexual revolution has come. Until 1954, female civil servants in the Netherlands would be dismissed from their jobs upon marriage.

Ayaan had a sister, Haweya, initially a rebellious girl who wore short skirts to provoke her parents and family circle. Wishing to escape a forced marriage, she joined her sister in the Netherlands. "But," explains Buruma, "it was as if a life of rebelliousness had taken too great a toll." After arriving in the Western country, she began to wear a hijab; she ultimately returned to Kenya after suffering an episode of depression. She developed paranoia and stopped eating. She died in 1998. Ayaan took the opposite path. The guilt she felt when she rejected the chains that bound her to her past (the hijab, the prohibition on alcohol, the requirement of chastity, halal) was transformed into a militant atheism. In Theo van Gogh she had found a brother-in-arms.

The desire for strict religious rules that overcame Ayaan's sister is a form of nostalgia, a way of reappropriating the world of one's parents, of fighting against the "bewildering maelstrom of Western temptations." Jihadists, wandering in a world where they have lost their frames of reference, paradoxically return to their origins, in a bizarre fabrication that stupefies their parents. When questioned about how their children drifted toward jihadism, the parents are the first to express surprise. They almost always say, over and over again: "We don't understand, he wasn't observant, he drank, he went to night clubs." These (paradoxical) statements serve to contradict those who would doubt the sincerity of children's desire for integration.

Olivier Roy has provided a very illuminating analysis of the sociology of the jihadists.[14] They are often second-generation immigrants, and a quarter of them are converts to Islam. Fairly well integrated at first, they later pass through a phase of petty criminal behavior, followed by a radicalization in prison. They are "born again": After a secular life (of alcohol and girls), they abruptly feel the need for a religious practice. The transition to the "religious" occurs outside the mosque and the Muslim community. Sponsors of jihad in fact define it as an individual obligation. "Jihad must be practiced by the child himself if his parents refuse."

The French debate on the causes of jihadism is profoundly marked by a quarrel between Olivier Roy and Gilles Kepel. Roy believes that the radicalization of some young people leads them to seize on Islam as a means of revolt, whereas Kepel makes the opposite argument: Islam, by way of Salafism, is responsible for that radicalization. Farhad Khosrokhavar, having conducted a vast international comparison, provides very useful keys for resolving this controversy.[15] In France, he writes, "the Islamization of radicalism" is much more common, especially among the young in the suburbs. The opposite is true in other countries, such as England, Holland, Norway, Denmark, and Canada, where community structures are better preserved. In these cases, the radicalization of Islam is the dominant feature.

In France, according to Khosrokhavar, "secular culture and republican schooling have contributed to de-Islamizing young Maghrebis, which for many individuals has increased the appeal of a mythified Islam." This phenomenon leads Olivier Roy to draw a parallel between the terrorist actions of the jihadists and those of the Far Left in the seventies. In his view, there is a continuity between present-day jihadists and the Red Brigades, the Baader-Meinhof gang, and the Japanese Red Army of that time. All sought radicalism for its own sake, just as anarchists in the late nineteenth century had previously done. For the jihadists, Islam plays the role of a fantasy in the same way that the October Revolution did for the Far Left in May '68. Andreas Baader was not a proletarian, no more were the shooters at the Bataclan theater devout militants. Jean-Marc Rouillan, a former member of the defunct Far-Left group Action Directe, which committed two murders in France, expressed his "admiration" for the courage of the Bataclan shooters. Carlos, a Venezuelan terrorist who planned some of the attacks of the seventies and eighties, converted to Islam in prison. The members of the Baader-Meinhof gang blamed their parents for their complicity with Nazism. The children of Algerians do not understand how the heroic saga of the National Liberation Front (FLN) could have ended in social servitude. In both cases, the parents are reproached for their failures, and the children throw the martyrdom of their own lives back in their parents' faces.

THE THIRD AGE OF VIOLENCE

Nevertheless, the key phenomenon that governs our understanding of jihadist violence, and which radically distinguishes it from that of the seventies, is that, since the early nineties, the civil violence has diminished everywhere. By 1999 it had dropped to its 1966 level, and in 2010 it was down even further, to a historic low. According to Steven Pinker, who analyzed the sharp rise of violence in the sixties, a re-civilizing process has been set in motion. The increase in homicides that began in the sixties lasted three decades. From the mid-nineties on, violence dropped as quickly as it had risen.

Several hypotheses have been put forward to explain this change. For Steven Levitt, author of the best seller *Freakonomics*, it is the deferred consequence of the legalization of abortion in the seventies: With the reduction in the number of unplanned pregnancies coming to term, the criminality of adolescents whose parents had not wanted them disappeared. No one now really believes that hypothesis, because, among other things, violence abated everywhere in the world, regard-less of whether abortion was legal. In addition, some have advanced the idea that a more systematic incarceration policy ultimately bore fruit. Almost 2 million Americans are now behind bars, that is, about 6 percent of the active popula-tion for each age brackets. The problem is that prison turns out to be a two-edged sword: It can also radicalize inmates. The jihadists are examples of that paradoxical effect. In the case of Black Americans, incarceration has primarily had the toxic effect of leaving a number of single-parent families to fend for themselves. That does not mean that it is better to let crimes go unpunished. But the proof that imprisonment is not directly responsible for the drop in criminality is that Canada, which did not follow that policy, recorded the same change as the United States. Finally, the idea that the cause may have been the resumption of economic growth seen in the nineties does not stand up to scrutiny. The downward trend continued during the Great Recession of 2008.

It seems that a process exactly symmetrical to that of the sixties is under way. It can be seen as a delayed effect of the counterculture that arose at the time. Initially violent, a reac-tion to contemporary society, it gradually changed in nature as it made inroads in public opinion. The insistence on the civil rights of minorities, the fight to end violence against women, in short, the respect for differences, racial or sexual, produced a reduction in interpersonal violence. The pacifica-tion of society has finally come, resulting from the spread of an ethical code of tolerance and respect for others champi-oned in the sixties.

The sociologist Cas Wooters speaks of a third age of vio-lence.[16] The first is described by Hobbes, that of Europe in the seventeenth century, where you could kill your neighbors if they insulted you. The second age was that described by Elias, when the state acquired the monopoly on legitimate violence. The third age, which we have now entered, is that of a "controlled decontrolling of emotions." We now cast a distant and controlling gaze on violence. Women's short skirts and men's profane language no longer carry the meaning they once did. They are not taken at face value as signs of moral deviation or vulgarity. We play around with past norms, unafraid of the consequences that deviance from them used to have. Society has become sufficiently civilized to allow us to have some fun with the codes of violence, without fearing that we will get caught up in it.

That "euphemization" of violence does not mean it is disappearing. Behind the reassuring statistics of a decline in homicides, the violence young people commit against themselves remains of considerable scope. The practice of binge drinking, for example, has never been more prevalent.[17] In an article devoted to the lifestyle and health of the young, Fabrice Étilé examines the high-risk behavior of young people and its link to their social background.[18] Since time immemorial, adolescents have had intense emotional reactions, which can be explained by the novelty of the situations they encounter and a greater sensitivity to stimuli. This explains their increased appetite for high-risk activities, such as extreme sports, excessive speed, theft, or the use of drugs (Françoise Dolto makes this point in *Championing the Cause of Adolescents*).[19]

What interests Étilé is the way social differences find expression in this regard. Analyzing tobacco consumption, he shows that middle-class young people engage in high-risk behavior when they are adolescents but become more sensible when they enter adulthood. In working-class milieus, the opposite is the case. For lack of money, young people from disadvantaged areas begin to smoke later in life than young bourgeois. But when these underprivileged youth start earning a living, fewer of them quit smoking. Étilé—an ironic economist—concludes quite simply that the value of life is lower for the working classes.

This comparison sheds light on the difference between the violence of the seventies and that of the present. The first-wave terrorists were restrained by an instinct for self-preservation, which those of the second lack. Earlier terrorists often came from the upper classes: They pounded their fists to transform the world in their image. Alan Krueger shows that they were better educated on average than the rest of the population. He even lists several billionaires in his data.[20] The majority of jihadists come from the working class or lower middle classes. Their social environment and their motivations are very different from those of their predecessors. The nihilism of the jihadists, who often seek death in defiance of any "operational" rationale, is the sign of a total loss of confidence in Western society's capacity to respond to their aspirations.

There is one zone, however, where violence continues to thrive regardless of the environment, namely, the cultural zone. Already in the nineteenth century, "crime novels" had become a way for readers to entertain the fear (and attraction) of violence, even as that violence was receding in reality. As Pinker says, the Rolling Stones would now look like a charitable organization when compared to the violence of punk, metal, goth, grunge, gangsta rap, and hip-hop. Social networks have also become a morass of hatred. Behind the cover of online aliases, Internet users attack the most innocuous sites. A highly respected American magazine devoted to popular science had to shut down its Web site because it was flooded with hateful criticism. The violence of what is called *cyberbullying* in the United States has also had many victims. Two-thirds of the young people bullied on social networks have attempted suicide, according to the psychologist Jean Twenge.[21]

ISIL has taken possession of the Internet in its own way. Its filmmaking style is directly inspired by video games. Its recruits are digital natives of the Western world, who are promised a place in paradise, but also and above all, a place in the digital imaginary. This, Antonio Quinet says that "Screens nowadays favor the instinctual aspect of images, excluding reflection through culture and civilization."[22] The perpetrator of a 2016 truck attack in the city of Nice took a selfie just before beginning his deadly rampage. This use of technology gives an additional specificity to the jihadists. Even while laying claim to a lost world of faith and tradition, they have ready access to hypermodernity, that of video games and social networks. In their desperate way, they serve as a bridge between the two worlds.

PART III

Back to the Future

CHAPTER SIX

The Great Hope of the Twenty-First Century

AS INDUSTRIAL SOCIETY was collapsing, the ascent of digital society irresistibly continued. The mythologies—the grand narratives that sustain the new world—owe a great deal to the ideals that made their first appearance in the sixties. Mark Zuckerberg, the founder of Facebook, likes to style himself as an heir to the underground culture of hackers that arose in the United States in the sixties. In the seventies, the university and its youth-centered culture were a remarkable platform for the spread of the computer revolution. To its pioneers, that culture looked like a space of freedom embodying an ideal of horizontality and access free of charge. For the sociologist Manuel Castells, protest culture provided students who grew up on American campuses the means to shatter the standardization of the world created by their parents. "The universities," he writes, "were the principal agents of diffusion and social innovation. The young people who attended them discovered and adopted new ways of thinking, acting, and communicating."[1] As the historian François Caron would also say, "The antiestablishment hedonism of the sixties was realized in the technologization of society in the seventies and eighties."[2]

The libertarian ideal of a nonhierarchical society, where all people have access to a power that frees them from large industrial institutions, is indisputably part of the legacy of the sixties. It propagated the idea that the new world would mark the coming of a society that has finally been humanized—the revenge, in the economic realm, of Sartre over Lévi-Strauss. That expectation was also expressed earlier. Back in 1948, Jean Fourastié's *Great Hope of the Twentieth Century* provided a brilliant anticipation of the world to come. Fourastié explains that, after agrarian societies, which cultivated the soil, then industrial society, which worked matter, in the service society human beings would finally cultivate themselves. Education, health, and leisure would be central to the new world.

Fourastié thus declares that "the civilization of the tertiary sector will be brilliant; half or three-quarters of the population will enjoy the advantages of higher education. Within a few generations, initiative even in low-skill work, and the diversity of the means of transportation and of leisure activities, will favor the individualist tendencies of human beings." Therefore, he concludes, "the time is coming when history will have advanced far enough that human beings can legitimately endeavor to elaborate the philosophy of the new age, and work in a less oppressive darkness toward a dramatic birth. In liberating humanity from the labor that inanimate matter can execute on its behalf, the machine must lead us to jobs that, of all created beings, only human beings can perform: those of intellectual culture and moral improvement."[3] Léon Blum wrote an enthusiastic review of the book when it was published.

That transition to a "humanized" society gave rise to many commentaries, but all identified a central problem: It anticipated a world without growth. For Fourastié himself, there was no doubt that the service society, in no longer being subject to the invasion of machines, would make economic growth disappear. Without new technologies, wage stagnation became inevitable. All those with jobs in the service industry—the doctor who cares for a patient, the teacher in charge of a class, the actor who fills a theater—must deal with the absence of "economies of scale" that would allow a single service provider to reach an ever greater number of clients. The concept of economies of scale is fundamental in economic analysis. It describes the situation of a business that can increase its production without increasing its costs, or by increasing them only a little. This allows the business to set in motion a "virtuous circle": The larger its customer base grows, the more the business thrives. Otherwise, beyond a certain size, it is condemned to stagnate.[4] If the maximum benefit from such economies of scale is to be achieved, new technologies that can increase the producers' impact are needed. Film and television, for example, have allowed actors to perform before ever greater numbers of viewers. It is possible that the digital revolution is now offering a solution of the same nature to the service society as a whole. When a watch on my wrist analyzes my pulse, temperature, and red blood cell count, then a "customized" solution to my health problems can be developed by an algorithm (and, in unusual circumstances, by a human being, if the algorithm judges one necessary). It therefore really is human beings who are central to postindustrial society, but human beings who must be digitized beforehand if the inexhaustible thirst for growth in modern societies is to be satisfied.

The Robot Who Loved Me

The film *Her*, set in the 2020s, tells the story of a man abandoned by his wife, who falls in love with a computer program. The film, directed by Spike Jonze in 2013, sums up with poetic humor the culmination of the digital revolution, when the world of flesh and blood will merge with algorithms.

The film's success lies in its meticulous depiction of the mechanisms that make this unlikely story credible. The software speaks with the bewitching voice of Scarlett Johansson, the unforgettable star of *Lost in Translation* and *Match Point*. She seduces Theodore (Joaquin Phoenix) by whispering words of love, by taking him for a walk in the city, by telling him stories he finds delightful. When the body urgently imposes its demands, Samantha recruits a woman to make love in her place. The woman remains silent: It is Samantha who speaks, who murmurs her love for him. Theodore, obliged to confess to his co-worker that his girlfriend is software, cannot decline an outing with his co-worker's fiancée. She asks Samantha whether it bothers her not to have a body. To which Scarlett replies, tit for tat: "I'm not tethered to time and space in the way that I would be if I was stuck inside a body that's inevitably going to die." Everyone laughs awkwardly.

The story ends when Theodore discovers that Samantha is in other relationships, that she has millions of lovers at once. This betrayal makes the viewer realize all at once what we expect from a person we love: a love affair that is unique in our hearts and in the lover's as well. The program is not a person, less because she does not have a physical body than because she can form a bond with anyone. At the end of the film, it is actually Samantha who leaves Theodore. In cyberspace, she has discovered a superior program that has created a community, a software cult, much more interesting than the human community. She leaves Theodore to his loneliness as a finite, imperfect, incomplete being.

What seems to be an entertaining parody of the contemporary world proves to be a remarkable analysis of its potentialities. Samantha, with her millions of lovers, provides the key: Computers make it possible to increase the efficiency of interpersonal relationships. The psychoanalyst Serge Tisseron has written a captivating book in which he reveals the film's profundity.[5] From a technical standpoint, there are already emotional apps. The American psychologist Paul Ekman, one of the pioneers in facial recognition software, inspired a number of firms, such as Emotient Inc. and Affectiva Inc., whose products allow a computer to identify the emotions of a human being. The software will therefore be able to say: "You seem upset, is it because your wife hasn't come home?" It records your face, your respiration rate. The robot can match the tone of its voice to that of its interlocutor, as Samantha does. When Theodore is joyful, so is she. She affects a pure and complicitous voice, adapted to the expectations of her interlocutor in every respect and in all circumstances. "This film," concludes Tisseron, "is a parable of a man's loneliness in the face of a machine with the capacity to attune itself perfectly to his internal states. Because in reality he is conversing only with himself."

To be interesting, the robot will learn as well to finesse "relatively" unpredictable but always acceptable reactions, in order to surprise and seduce. Robots might well relieve humans of their everyday disappointments with other humans. They can become "allies of the fear of others." The fantasy of exerting absolute dominion over other people (as de Sade described it) would be given free rein. All social existence rests to a (varying) degree on the sublimation and dissimulation of one's true feelings. Robots will play a role in regulating them.

The question is not whether robots will one day have emotions similar to our own. It is whether we humans are ready to feel affection for them. Everything suggests that we are. Soldiers in the US Army became attached to the robots assigned to secure minefields in the place of humans. Once a robot saves a soldier's life, the soldier becomes irresistibly attached to it, sometimes putting himself in danger to recover it. Being able disconnect robots is not enough to overcome this feeling. To get over them, we will have to want to do so.

The psychoanalyst Donald Winnicott's analysis of children's attachment to their "loveys," which he calls "transitional objects," illustrates the psychological mechanism at work. These objects (blankets, teddy bears, and so on) guarantee "the transition between the time when the child expects everything from its mother and the time when it will agree not to be systematically satisfied by her." Normally, attachment to the "lovey" lasts only until the child agrees to give up the exclusive and tyrannical relationship it had first established with its mother, or with the person who takes her place. As children grow up, the relationship to objects is supposed to change. At different stages of life, objects become accomplices in our actions and our relationships with others. For Tisseron, it would be very surprising if robots did not acquire a status at least equivalent to the automobile, which drivers religiously wash on Sunday. They allow us to "totally control an object, to the point of calmly entrusting all or part of ourselves to it." The attachment to robots, he adds, is reinforced by "the general tendency of human beings to attribute to their whole environment intentions, emotions, even thoughts similar to their own."

Human beings were for a long time "animists," persuaded that animals and the forests were the bodies and dwellings of the gods. It took the Neolithic Revolution, the invention of agriculture, for humans to allow themselves to domesticate animals and cultivate the earth. They could do so only if they changed their gods; they had to worship new ones who blessed animal husbandry. Now human beings have embarked on a new psychological revolution, when they will be tempted to attribute a soul to machines that they themselves have built.

Homo Digitalis

Ultimately, the revolution we are going through is of recent date.

Its origin lies in the US Defense Advanced Research Projects Agency. In 1969 this agency set up a revolutionary communications network, whose object was to protect the American communications system from the risks of a Soviet military strike. That network gradually came to be used by academics under contract with the Pentagon. It entered the public domain thanks to the invention of the modem in 1978, by two students at the University of Chicago, who wanted to communicate for free, outside the Department of Defense server. A year later, in 1979, three students from Duke University and the University of North Carolina developed a modified version of Unix[6] that could link up computers through a simple telephone line. Thanks to the concomitant progress in fiber optics, the technology for transmitting digital packets took off. The Internet came into being thanks to these developments, potentially linking all computers on the planet by phonelines.

One cannot help but be fascinated by the speed at which the transformation of the digital world occurred. In 1989 Tim Berners-Lee and Robert Cailliau designed the World Wide Web. In 1994 Jeff Bezos created Amazon. In 1997 Deep Blue, an IBM computer, beat the world chess champion, Garry Kasparov. In 1998 Sergey Brin and Larry Page founded Google.

In 1999 Interbrand introduced Wi-Fi. In 2000 Bill Clinton authorized the use of GPS for civilian purposes. In 2003 the complete sequencing of the human genome was achieved. In 2005 Jawed Karim posted online a video called "Me at the Zoo" and invented YouTube. In 2006 Jack Dorsey sent the first "tweet" via Twitter, a technology he had created. The same year, Facebook, until then reserved for students, became accessible to everyone. In 2007 Steve Jobs introduced the iPhone, in 2010 the iPad. In 2012 a neural implant allowed a patient with spinal cord paralysis to operate a robotic arm with his thoughts. In 2018 an implant in the brain of a quadriplegic let him operate with his thoughts an exoskeleton that helped him walk.[7]

In 2006 the computer program AlphaGo, developed by DeepMind Technologies, a subsidiary of Google, beat one of the best Go players in the world, the Korean Lee Sedol; a year later, it defeated the world champion, Ke Jie. Three hundred million players followed the match live. The software won with an eccentric, totally unusual move. The former champion, dumbfounded, had to leave the room and get control of himself before making the next move. In China, Go is considered the fourth essential art, after painting, calligraphy, and qin music. The number of combinations in this game is infinitely greater than the number of atoms in the universe. It was certainly to be predicted that artificial intelligence would one day beat the best players, but no one thought it would happen so quickly. And the surprises do not end there. A year later, DeepMind Technologies designed a new program, AlphaGo Zero, which beat the previous software. Incredibly, it had learned to play on its own, training against itself.

Progress in artificial intelligence reached a critical new phase after discoveries allowed it to imitate the structure of the human brain's neural pathways. This method is behind the successes of AlphaGo Zero. Unlike first-generation artificial intelligence, the procedure does not consist of entering, from an already-existing library, all the matches played by humans, in order to find the best moves. The software learns on its own, playing against itself, first as a novice, then with greater and greater skill. It uses its own "synapses," its own memory, to acquire experience, until it outperforms human beings, thanks to strategies that no one had previously thought of. This method already allows artificial intelligence to recognize skin cancers better (and more quickly) than the best specialists. But it is also behind the discovery of twenty-five hundred exoplanets, some in a solar system that greatly resembles our own.

The human brain, whose modes of operation artificial intelligence seeks to copy, contains as many neurons as there are stars in our galaxy, about 100 billion. Each is connected to a thousand others through junctions called *synapses*, used with varying frequency and at different intensities. The unused links are eliminated; inversely, when two neurons are stimulated at the same time, connections uniting them are created or reinforced. What matters is less the number of neurons than the quality of the connections between them.[8] The traces remaining of the neural links that have marked our lives form the basis of our memory and personality.

What is known as *deep learning* artificial intelligence was inspired by the neural networks of the human brain. Every time the computer discovers a strategy that allows it to progress (toward winning a game of Go, for example), it remembers the winning connections and, like a human being, is able to construct an experience curve. One of the pioneers in the field, the Frenchman Yann LeCun, who now works for Facebook, developed such neural pathways to design a system that automatically recognizes signatures on checks. In 2012 the Canadian physicist Geoffrey Hinton made use of deep learning to win an international image recognition competition. He was quickly snatched up by Google for the Google Brain project. This was the start of an influx of researchers pursuing this method. In 2014 the DeepFace project, a Facebook program, succeeded in recognizing an individual in two different photos with a success rate of 97.35 percent, the same as a human being. Facebook, which has in its possession the largest gallery of photos in the world, can now find, apparently with a high rate of success, friends with whom we might have lost touch.

Where will these revolutions lead us? To borrow the title of Yuval Noah Harari's *Homo deus*, the next stage anticipated is quite simply that human beings will become God, that they will prevail over death, by merging human intelligence with artificial intelligence software.[9] "The cyborg race will fuse the organic body with nonorganic devices, such as bionic hands, artificial eyes, or millions of nanorobots that will navigate our blood vessels, diagnose problems, and repair the damage." Craig Venter, founder of Celera Corporation, a specialist in genetic research who was criticized for "playing God," is said to have replied: "We're not playing!" The futurist Ray Kurzweil, who left MIT for Google, is famous for having taken that idea to the extreme. He predicts that, by 2045, there will be nothing less than an abrupt evolutionary transition by the human race, when the biological will merge with silicon.[10]

Digital Utopia

Larry Page, Elon Musk, and Peter Thiel are billionaires who want to be the pioneers in this new world. They are all digital utopians inspired by the futurist Hans Moravec. In *Mind Children*, Moravec foresees a world in which the human race will be swept aside by its own progeny, intelligent machines. "Unleashed from the plodding pace of biological evolution, the children of our minds will be free to grow to confront immense and fundamental challenges in the larger universe. We humans will benefit for a time from their labors, but sooner or later, like natural children, they will seek their own fortunes while we, their aged parents, silently fade away."[11]

Max Tegmark, a professor of physics at MIT and a specialist in artificial intelligence (who can therefore not be accused of speaking from ignorance), paints a glowing picture of the process under way. In the prologue to *Life 3.0*, he describes the stages that will allow, credibly in his view, the software, "Prometheus," to conquer the world. [12] In the first place, it could get rich, by selling software or technical innovations to businesses or individuals, then by investing that money in the stock market, an exercise in which it would outperform the usual traders. It could also produce films, with actors it would have fabricated itself; by analyzing the library of all existing films and studying the critics, it would learn how to make the perfect movie. With its talent and money, it could then buy major media to defend an agenda based on lower taxes, open borders, lower military expenditures, and praise of the "free press." It would become master of the world and of the world's ideologies.

For Tegmark, also inspired by Moravec, we are heading toward a third age of intelligence. The first, which he calls Life 1.0, appeared on earth 4 billion years ago, when "intelligent" bacteria succeeded in acquiring information about their environment, which allowed them to optimize their response to it. They were not equipped with any capacity for evolution. Their DNA (the "hardware") established the limits of their possibilities. Then came Life 2.0, in the form of *Homo sapiens*, some hundreds of thousands of years ago. Its "hardware" consisted of relatively unsophisticated DNA: it contained one gigabit of information, the equivalent of a movie download. The strength of human intelligence is that, during a person's lifetime, it is able to store an infinitely greater quantity of information thanks to the synapses it uses: to learn French or mathematics. Human "hardware" is fixed, but the "software" gives it considerable flexibility. Language, writing, printing, science, computers, and the Internet constitute the long succession of innovations that subsequently allowed an exponential accumulation of collective human knowledge.

Whatever the intelligence accumulated by humans, it is still limited by the biological "hardware." No one can live a million years or learn Wikipedia by heart. It is this limitation that Life 3.0 will eradicate, according to Tegmark. The "software" will be able to redefine the "hardware." Intelligence will be able to migrate from the human body to silicon. There is, he adds, no (known) law of physics that prevents a computer from performing better than a human brain. Sunway TaihuLight, the most powerful computer in existence, already has the computational capacity of a human brain. It has a 300 million dollar price tag: for the moment, a human being costs less.[13] But if we try to extrapolate from what the laws of physics allow us to imagine (including the quantum computers in development), we can anticipate, according to Tegmark, that the cost of calculations will be divided by ten.[33] At the current rate, it will still take two centuries to arrive at that point.

Artificial intelligence has already made considerable progress in perception and cognition, two areas in which human beings were deemed unbeatable. Voice recognition and translation capacities have evolved a great deal. To be convinced of that, we need only provide a text to be translated into Chinese, then have it retranslated from Chinese back into English. There are still some mistakes, but the effect is impressive. Errors in photo recognition have fallen from 30 percent in 2010 to 2.2 percent in 2017. The software can now recognize a cat, which was apparently the holy grail for computer scientists. An audacious parallel has been drawn to what is called the "Cambrian explosion" 500 million years ago, the big bang of earthly life, when forms of life proliferated. The cause may have been the sense of sight. If machines too could see and share their knowledge with other machines, a revolutionary change would indisputably be at work.

Clearly, there is always a point where fantasy gets the better of reality. When transhumanism announces that it will be able to conquer death by fusing man and machine, it crosses a line that few scientists agree to cross. As the two great brain specialists Danièle Tritsch and Jean Mariani show, aging is unavoidable, though there are realistic hopes that we will die in better health.[14] The problem with neurons is that they do not renew themselves. They are the same age as the individual in whom they are housed and retain the traces of an eventful life.[15] If current trends continue, in 2070 life expectancy will be ninety years for men and ninety-three for women. There is little reason to think we could do much better than that. The number of very old people has stagnated since the eighties. Jeanne Calment's record, 122 years old, has never been broken. In 2017 there were 77 women and 2 men over 110 years old, and that number is not rising. "Come on now," Mariani and Tritsch conclude, "transhumanism is a sham. Humans as we know them, with their strengths and weaknesses, still have good days ahead of them." As the philosopher Francis Wolff puts it poetically: "We must die, and there is nothing about this that should terrify us. But humanity must not die, and that is something around which to rally our remaining hopes."[16]

The (immediate) question, however, is not whether man will become a machine, or whether robots might one day have our ability to feel emotions, to be afraid of dying, for example, as in the film *Blade Runner*.[17] The question is what robots will be able to do better and more cheaply than humans. Artificial intelligence is already infinitely superior to human intelligence at doing calculations. It can multiply in a microsecond numbers larger than those that humans will ever have occasion to handle. But there are many tasks for which humans will remain indispensable, if only because the users of the new technologies, the clients, are also humans with a human sensibility. The whole question is how to come to an understanding about what the division of labor will be, and how to understand the extent to which the promise of a humanization of the productive world will emerge intact from that new confrontation between human beings and their creations.

The Robot and the Devil

The term *robot* was invented in 1924 by the science fiction author Karel Čapek, to designate a machine that could not be distinguished from a human.[18] Richard Freeman, professor at Harvard and one of the undisputed specialists on the labor market, wrote a provocative article called "Who Owns the Robots Rules the World," in which he announced a remarkable transformation of the world of work.[19] In this world, the owners of robots will earn a growing share of global revenue. The oldest questions of human history have made a brutal resurgence: Will machines destroy employment? In what tasks will humans specialize?

The list of advances that software has made is dizzying. It is now possible to hold a microchip the size of a grain of rice between the thumb and index finger and follow Alzheimer's patients remotely or identify oneself to a robot. A patient whose right hand was amputated tested a prothesis, linked by electrodes to the nerves in his forearm, that restored his sense of touch. Neural machine translation has achieved an accuracy

still unthinkable even a few years ago. Artificial intelligence
will allow us to speak with someone speaking Chinese, by
means of a simultaneous translation system working through
an earpiece. IBM Watson, the office assistant endowed with
artificial intelligence, makes short work of the information
contained in Wikipedia and can give an informed opinion in
an increasingly wide range of professions (law, teaching). It is
already analyzing, at a higher rate of efficiency than specialists, the medical files of patients with tumors. Another appli-
cation now available is Genie MD, which allows patients to
do a self-diagnosis and so manage common problems, with
professionals later following up on the complicated cases.[20]
And, as everyone knows, the self-driving car is coming soon.
All the automobile manufacturers are involved in research
making driverless cars possible. General Motors signed a draft
agreement with IBM, Ford with Google. Toyota is also in on
the action; its objective is to launch reliable models by 2020.
In the United States, self-driving cars and trucks threaten the
livelihood of 4.1 million truck drivers.

The mounting fear that machines will replace human
beings is not new, of course. The French demographer Alfred
Sauvy, in *Unemployment and the Machine*, has painted a
remarkable sketch of that trepidation.[21] Every new machine,
from the pulley the Romans used to lift columns to Vaucan-
son's power looms, incited the dread that human labor would
disappear. The fear that one day, as Simonde de Sismondi said
at the dawn of the nineteenth century, "the king, by constantly
turning a crank, will produce all the work of England by means
of automatons," is among the age-old fears that economists
ordinarily find annoying (quoted by Sauvy). In their eyes,
exactly the opposite is true: Technical progress is the ultimate
source of growth, which is always good for jobs. The idea that
technical progress can destroy employment is in fact refuted

by even the most cursory glance at the data. During the Glorious Thirty the labor force became twice as productive, and hiring was never so sustained. Conversely, economists generally interpret the rise of unemployment in the seventies and eighties as one of the effects of a slowdown in technological progress, not its acceleration.

The slowing of employment preoccupies economists less than the slowing of growth.[22] Fourastié predicted it. The growth associated with the mechanization of agriculture and then of industry had to end, as society shifted to a service economy. In a famous statement, he pointed out that we are now incomparably richer when measured in kilos of wheat consumed or in household appliances, but still just as poor when measured in haircuts. According to him, a lower rate of growth is the necessary counterpart to the transition to a service economy. It is the price to be paid for social tranquility. The doctor who puts her ear to a patient's chest and prescribes the right medication is in the realm of the "F2F," face-to-face. She practices her profession in a world without economies of scale: Each doctor cares for a more or less fixed number of patients.

Fourastié's view must be reformulated, however, if we are to have a better grasp of the changes in employment. Let us begin by distinguishing three stages in the productive process: the design of the commodity, its production, and its prescribed use. In a postindustrial society, the production phase disappears: It costs (almost) nothing to produce goods. The economy thus brings together two terms that are somewhat at odds: the design of the commodity (the immaterial) and its prescribed use (its marketing). Let us reconsider the medical example. The chemical formula of a medication is immaterial. The design process can take advantage of significant economies of scale: All human beings benefit from the medication.

Production itself costs less and less (the price of generics is low). The last stage is the prescribed use, the face-to-face relationship with the doctor, the stage Fourastié privileged.

This description gives a glimpse of a potential solution to the problem of growth. In this example, technical advances, by making innovations, developing new drugs, make doctors more efficient in the treatment of patients. Complementarity between the design and the prescribed use can increase the productivity of service jobs. Unfortunately, what has become evident in the last twenty years is that this is not an accurate assessment of the situation. The jobs oriented toward human beings (educators, aides for the elderly) have become much less lucrative. They do not glow with the radiant future of the world of work. The promises of a society propelled by the world of services, where everyone is someone else's psychoanalyst or beautician, have been clouded by the phenomenon that economists have called *job polarization*. Jobs with large economies of scale, those of Silicon Valley geeks, the "symbol manipulators" to borrow Robert Reich's expression, have grown considerably more lucrative, as have financiers and great artists. F2F jobs have remained plentiful, but the pay is very bad.[23]

Several phenomena account explain why service jobs lost status.[24] First, they received the overflow of workers whose jobs in the other sectors were destroyed. As the jobs associated with the old industrial world have been eliminated in factories or management, those who formerly held them have turned in growing numbers to service jobs. The indirect result is a reduction in pay. But another, more insidious factor has also played a role. With digitization, a number of tasks have been subcontracted to consumers themselves, who use software to perform them. Computers now make it possible to do all sorts of transactions online that in the past would have required the services of a salaried employee. Everything that does not benefit economies of scale tends to be transferred to consumers, who are now responsible for repairing their own televisions, buying tickets online, and soon, taking care of themselves on their own. In the future, 3D printers will also allow them to produce at home the products they need. This development represents a tremendous reversal of the trends operative in the sixties. Formerly, washing machines liberated women from a household chore, encouraging them to join the labor market and emancipate themselves from their husband's guardianship. Now software has consumers themselves performing tasks that used to be paid work.

Whatever its origin, the pressure exerted on (remunerated) work has translated to an unprecedented fall in wages in favor of capital income. In analyzing in detail the causes of that development, economists have noted a significant change. The most successful companies, the top five in each sector, have considerably increased their market share. But, with the exception of the finance sector, these businesses are much more frugal in their labor costs than their competitors. This is a widespread phenomenon. Whatever the sector considered, the fewer employees a firm has, the greater its success. Erik Brynjolfsson and his coauthors speak of "scale without mass."[25] The model of the "superstar firm" is taking root, along with a recurrent feature, that of "winner takes most." Netflix and Google can double their sales without doubling their staff. What is surprising is that this model seems to be establishing itself everywhere, not just in the sector of digital industries. In the United States, the top hundred companies formerly produced a third of aggregate value added. Their share has now risen to 50 percent.

In industry, retail trade, and the hotel business, the share of the leading firm continues to grow and, in every case, the number of salaried employees in each case is lower relative to sales.[26] Currently, the financial sector is the exception to the rule that salaries are in decline vis-à-vis value added or sales. But that, no doubt, is only a matter of time. In the polarization of postindustrial employment, it is truly jobs with strong economies of scale that are prevailing. The other jobs are drop down the pecking order, because they are confined to the realm that Fourastié heralded as emancipatory, F2F, the old person-to-person relationship.

This is a long way from the ideal promised by the computer revolution at its inception. Disappointment is nothing new, however. When electricity was invented, there was a belief that it would save the mass of small factories that were still feeding industrial production. They didn't have their own power sources and were subjected to the inexorable competition of the large facilities with steam engines. Zola was a witness to that expectation: after writing *The Beast Within*, he composed *Labor*, a little-known novel that is a paean to electricity. But electricity betrayed that hope. Making it easier to regulate and partition the production process, it ultimately gave birth to assembly-line work in very large facilities and sealed the fate of the small factories.[27]

Digital society has dashed a similar expectation. Once again, the promise of an economy on a human scale, of "small is beautiful," has not been kept. If we compare the leading triumvirate of the present time (Google, Apple, and Amazon) to the top companies of the past (General Motors and Chrysler in their glory), we find that their market capitalization is nine times higher than that of their predecessors, but with one-third the work force.

It is truly the evaporation of well-paid jobs that stokes everyone's fears.

Two Possible Worlds

What will labor become in the digitized world? Must we adopt the fears of those who once again predict its disappearance or at least its loss of status? Back in the nineties, Jeremy Rifkin, in his best seller *The End of Work*, wrote that the information age is at our fingertips.[28] Intelligent machines were replacing human beings in an infinite number of jobs, relegating millions of white- and blue-collar workers to the ranks of the unemployed, or worse, to bread lines. Through humanity's liberation from its most ancient and most natural burden, "the burden of laboring and the bondage to necessity," as Hannah Arendt wrote in a famous passage from *The Human Condition*, we would now be reaching an epilogue fraught with menace: the prospect of a society of workers without work, the worst thing imaginable.

The debate about the future of work often goes in circles. The errors of the past, those of the Luddites and of the Lyonnais silk workers who broke machines to save their jobs, will be thrown in the faces of the "pessimists." But it is just as easy to point out to the optimists their own errors. All the dams that were supposed to protect human labor have been blown up. The act of driving a car, which was considered too complicated to be left to a robot, is about to be automated. Empathy, which is supposed to be the exclusive realm of humans, has not prevented emotional robots from caring for the elderly in Japan.

As Daron Acemoglu and Pascual Restrepo remind us, nothing guarantees, theoretically or historically, that the process of digitization will ultimately be favorable to work.[29] It is not beside the point to recall that the first half of the nineteenth century was not particularly bright for the working class. Economic historians have shown that a long period of wage stagnation accompanied industrialization. Joel Mokyr describes that phenomenon as the "living standards paradox."[30] It was during this time that Marx was writing apocalyptic descriptions of factory life.

The timescale by which these transformations will be evaluated is obviously decisive. Within what framework will these changes take place? For the moment, digital society looks for the most part like an optimized continuation of industrial society. It has been the instrument of a widespread reduction of costs. "Uberization" has upended the organization of business and employees' circumstances, but an Uber driver's work is still to transport a customer. Digitization also allows us to manage the problems of interdependency that industrial society produced (traffic congestion, pollution), without really changing the model. The Airbnb or BlaBlaCar model can be understood as a way of saving, optimizing, the available resources—cars or accommodations—which remain the same as before. Ultimately, the end of postindustrial society would still be a pertinent question even if it were only a matter of regulating more efficiently the externalities of the old world.

It is possible, however, that with artificial intelligence and big data, a bifurcation is occurring. When taxis no longer have drivers, when people will be taken care of, educated, and entertained online without leaving their rooms, the world will have radically changed. Digital man will have created an entirely new society, of which he will be both the producer and the consumer. It is therefore possible to imagine two types of evolution, only one of which is reassuring. In the pessimistic version, the engineers, the "symbol manipulators," invent software, algorithms that keep a digital society running with an ever-smaller labor force. In this society of large and small "stars," the human labor force might become the domestic staff in the service of the elites. The Mark Zuckerbergs and Bill

Gateses will always need their barbers, doctors, and lawyers, who, in a domino effect, will offer lower and lower paying jobs to their own domestic staff. In this system, it will be a luxury to escape technologies and enjoy a personal service. But the farther one ventures from the top the more devalued employment will be and the more digitized the production of wealth.

There is a second possibility, in which man and machine discover new complementarities: The architect designs houses and has his clients visit them virtually, the professor reinvents her teaching methods, those in the health professions (doctors, pharmacists, nurses) prove capable of providing large-scale follow-ups to their patients, assisted by digital equipment, even while maintaining a significant human presence. According to David Autor, an American economist who has drawn attention to the polarization of employment, previous debates always held onto the fantasy of a perfect substitution of machine for man.[31] Yet history shows that complementarity between the two is more often the rule than the exception.

Economists speak of "general purpose technology" to characterize these disruptive technologies whose existence precedes the use that will be made of them.[32] The steam engine and electricity revolutionized the world in a way that extended far beyond their inventors' intentions. The steam engine was supposed to be used to pump water out of coal mines, not transport train passengers thousands of miles. Likewise, electricity was invented before radio, the washing machine, or television, about which Edison hadn't an inkling. For that matter, it is amusing to look at the misconceptions of these great inventors regarding the use of their inventions. Edison, for example, thought the gramophone would be used to record the last wills and testaments of the dying. Each of the innovations of previous times created growth, thanks to a series of later complementary inventions. Assembly-line work came into being because electricity made it possible to rethink the organization of labor "scientifically." The future of human work, its deskilling or, on the contrary, its upscaling, will depend on how society is able to imagine new complementarities between man and machines.

It is obviously too early to define precisely what that new division of labor might be. As David Autor points out, however, robots are comfortable primarily when surrounded by other robots. In factories, they can perform most of the tasks necessary for manufacturing a car because they operate in a perfectly programmed environment. Conversely, the garage mechanic who reinflates a tire or replaces a broken window must still be a human being. When it is necessary to act beyond the confines of a protocol, a human being is more suitable than a machine. By that argument, everything that can be codified by rules would fall to robots, everything that is discretionary would be the responsibility of humans. Robots excel at tasks that are circumscribed by a clear objective: to win or lose a game whose rules are perfectly well defined. Everything becomes more complicated when they are asked to do several things at once. Their capacity to arbitrate among contradictory imperatives is poor. As Yann LeCun points out, computers are lacking something like "common sense."[33]

Conversely, human beings are "multitaskers" at heart. They are body and mind. Even the barber in Fourastié's example does several things at once: cuts hair, keeps up a conversation, creates an environment that makes you want to come back. Specialists on microeconomics know it is very difficult to define an optimal program when several objectives have to be maximized. In the USSR, for example, when manufacturers were given instructions to produce as many busts of Lenin as possible, the busts all came out flimsy. When specifications were made that they be heavy, they became too heavy. When a problem is subtle and combines several objectives at once, it is inevitable that a program incapable of reasoning will privilege one objective at the expense of another.[34]

It is in situations of great ambiguity that robots fail. For example, a robot is incapable of distinguishing between the following statements: (1) The police denied unions the right to demonstrate because they feared violence; and (2) The police denied unions the right to demonstrate because they extolled violence. An intuitive interpretation of the statement allows a human being to understand who is doing what. One shudders to think of the consequences that a poor comprehension of the meaning of an instruction could have: nuclear war, a financial crisis, control tower errors, mistakes in drug tests.

But if robots are really comfortable only with other robots, the real risk is that human beings will have to adapt to the machine rather than vice versa. As Tisseron said, we must be wary of the human capacity to get used to robots, to settle into their rhythms and demands, in short, to become robots ourselves, not biologically but psychologically. Charlie Chaplin's *Modern Times* is a subtle illustration of this (perverse) capacity of human beings to submit to the imperatives of the machine. Transhumanists argue for a hybridization of humans and computers, the organic and the digital. In fact, that hybridization has already begun. The iPhone has become a new organ of the human body. The act of typing on our smartphones, constantly verifying that we have not missed a message, as if the device had become an integral part of our being both at work and at home, has become a wearisome tic of modern existence.

Although concern about the future of work and its hidden uncertainties obviously essential, the nature of the algorithmic world into which humans are slipping is the other unknown, the other face of the threat.

iGen

IN "RHIZOME," the introduction to *A Thousand Plateaus*, Gilles Deleuze and Félix Guattari provide a vision of a desirable world that seems to anticipate perfectly the hyperworld of the Internet.[1] "Rhizome" is defined in the Larousse dictionary as a perennial subterranean plant stem, generally close to horizontal, that annually produces roots below and shoots above. Deleuze and Guattari contrast the rhizome to the taproot, which creates shoots, creating many from one while the rhizome is multiple by nature. The root establishes a genealogy from one bifurcation to the next, whereas the rhizome is "antigenealogical," it has multiple entry points. It has no beginning or end, nothing but middle. "Make rhizomes, not roots, never plant!" They conclude that a nomadic, rhizomatic way of thinking must be set against "the logos, the philosopher king, the transcendence of the Idea, . . . the court of reason," as a machine of war against the hierarchical order.

The hypertextual world proposed by the Internet with its infinite ramifications perfectly fits the mold of that philosophical program. This is obviously not a matter of chance. The computer revolution is heir to the culture of the sixties.

Facebook styles itself a platform that allows everyone to create, in the form of networks, social environments by elective affinities, by proximity, without ever making use of visible hierarchies. We can all friend or unfriend as we like. Horizontality is the rule. The digital world imported (some of) its mythologies and counterculture from the sixties, to replace those that structured the industrial world, itself heir to a vertical and religious notion of society.

But what is the result? Is it a being emancipated from hierarchies, from the world of obedience that Deleuze and Guattari wanted to flee? On the contrary, it seems that the effort to participate in the network, to find one's place in it, to be recognized there, heralds a new servitude rather than the promise of liberation. In the great mirror of social networks, everyone seeks to magnify the construction of a being visible to others. Everyone wants to be beautiful, to have the largest number of friends, to constantly post images of the best things we are doing with our lives. A new "society of the spectacle" is coming into being. Andy Warhol declared in 1968: "In the future, everybody will be world-famous for fifteen minutes." As Bruno Patino and Jean-François Fogel note, the modern version of that prophecy could be that everyone will be famous for at least fifteen people.[2] Facebook does much better than that. An Internet user can count on several thousand friends, or so we all believe.[3]

Analyzing the profile of millennials, the generation born between 1980 and 2000, the newspaper *Les Échos* concludes that they consider their lives a story likely to interest others. This is a "superconnected" generation, whose members are "fans of Instagram and Snapchat, a generation worried about its image." About 95 million photos and videos are posted on Instagram every day. New beauty products—what L'Oréal calls "social beauty"—such as the "contour" cream popularized by

Kim Kardashian, enhance the complexion by catching the light optimally when a selfie is taken. Conversely, perfume, which cannot be captured in a photograph, is losing some of its importance. Millennials still sign off from social networks to go out on the town, but only on the condition that they have an "experience" they can then share with others. Restaurants are obliged to adopt the vogue for "food porn," which leads restaurateurs to focus on the use of color: Food must be beautiful to be loved. Peter Wells, food critic for the *New York Times*, worries that the good old grilled steak will ultimately disappear from menus because brown is not photogenic.

The invention of the iPhone in 2007 caused an acceleration in the trends created by the Internet, especially among the younger generations. In her book *iGen*, the psychologist Jean Twenge proposes a remarkable analysis of the generation's cultural practices.[4] The young people of iGen devote up to six hours a day to their devices: three hours to send and read texts or e-mails, the other half on social networks. Children sleep with their iPhones under their pillows or mattresses. Teenagers spend seventeen hours a day sleeping, going to school, and studying, while most of the rest of the time they spend with the new media.[5]

In their family lives, the members of iGen are victims of Tanguy syndrome, named for a French film whose eponymous hero does not want to leave the family home, thus exasperating his parents. The young are no longer in a rush to become adults, as those of the sixties could be. They no longer want to get away from their families as soon as possible: "iGen doesn't rebel against their parents' overprotection—instead, they embrace it." The journalist Raphaëlle Bacqué notes that "the family is no longer a problem today. More than that, the younger generations cite it as one of the most important elements from their point of view. Parents play the role of an administrative department that provides funding, consolation, repair services. A kind of safe haven."6

Safety is a key word that reflects this generation's obsessions. *Trauma* is another term often used (four times more often in 2005 than in 1965, according to the Google Books Database). It is necessary to distinguish here between the millennials and the next generation, iGen. The millennials are optimistic, displaying a certain confidence in themselves and in society. Arriving a decade later, iGen is more anxious, partly as a result of the recession. Its members have more difficulty expressing themselves in public (in class). They are preoccupied with succeeding in school. Like the millennials, however, the great division between the haves and the have-nots deeply disturbs iGen. They are more interested in the "extrinsic" values of success and money than in the "intrinsic" values, the satisfaction that an activity such as art or political engagement procures in and of itself.

Even as members of this generation make every effort to appear cheerful online, the flip side of social media is an underlying insecurity, fear of being rejected, of not being up to chasing the "awesome." The incidence of depression has greatly increased, especially among girls. "I spent hours watching perfect girls online, wishing I was them," one girl confided to Jean Twenge. Happiness does not seem to be meeting up with the connected life. A study titled "Internet and Life Satisfaction" indicates that the time spent on the Internet often correlates with sadness, a feeling of loneliness, lower levels of satisfaction. The study does not show that the Internet causes loneliness, however. It is altogether possible that the reverse is true, that loneliness and sadness about life result in frequent Internet use. But the experiments conducted tend to confirm that the Internet does play a causal role in reducing satisfaction.

Young people were asked to send a text message five times a day, in which they were to indicate whether they were happy or sad, and how much time they had spent on Facebook. It does appear that Facebook causes a drop in the sense of well-being. The more the young people used Facebook, the more unhappy they declared themselves to be; symptoms of depression rose after the user connected to the social network. A controlled study in Denmark points to the same trend. It divided a population into two groups: those deprived of Facebook and those who continued to use it. At the end of the week, those who had stopped using Facebook felt less lonely, less depressed, and happier.[7] Indeed, the social networks, despite their name, "desocialize" people. Facebook has a tendency to become an alternative to F2F encounters. The widespread use of the iPhone has led to a reduction in the number of outings with friends. According to Jean Twenge, the proportion of young people who go out with friends every day or almost every day has fallen from 50 percent to 25 percent.

iGen is establishing a strange relationship to politics. It seems to hesitate between apathy and radicalism ("political apathy and political polarization"). The social networks can disseminate to millions the image of a baby elephant embraced by its mother, but it can just as easily propagate a hate-filled radicalism. To the stupefaction of its designers, an artificial intelligence programmed to educate itself on the Internet independently became racist, repeating the stereotypes propagated by blogs dominated by white supremacists. The hesitation between indifference and radicalism can also be found in the relationship to political parties. An extraordinarily high number of young Americans (54 percent) say they are Independents rather than Democrats or Republicans. But at the same time, the number of those who say they are "on the Far Left" or "on the Far Right" is growing. They have risen from

13 percent in 1976 to 20 percent today. According to the Pew Research Center, animosity on the Left and the Right against the other side has continued to increase. Almost 58 percent of Republicans and 55 percent of Democrats harbor hatred for the other camp (versus 21 and 17 percent in 1994).

Donald Trump and Bernie Sanders appeal to American youth because they both look like outsiders in relation to the traditional political world. Trump beat Hillary Clinton because she was considered too close to the establishment. Sanders is attractive for the same reason. Young people's support for Sanders's "socialism" is fostered by a combinations of feelings: radical individualism and fear of economic insecurity. They are distrustful of government, yet they agree it should play a larger role in health and education.

Trust in the media and the educational system, which was excellent in the seventies (two-thirds of those polled had a favorable opinion), has also collapsed. A third of those surveyed have a favorable view of the media, less than half of the educational system. According to the General Social Survey, in 2014 only 21 percent of Americans trusted the basic institutions of American democratic life (the press, the school system, the Supreme Court). Jean Twenge makes a bitter diagnosis: iGen knows how to make videos but reads much less than previous generations, whether books or somewhat long articles.[8] Only 16 percent of adolescents read a book or magazine almost every day (versus a majority in the seventies). The proportion of those who read a newspaper at least once a week has dropped from 70 percent in the early seventies to 10 percent in 2015. The print media are disappearing. Two decades of the Internet have changed our relationship to reading more than millennia of writing.

A transformation in the relationship to time has also come about. Only 13 percent of young French people declare they would like to be living in future times.[9] Despite its enormous promises, the exponential development of technologies has not created a desire for what is to come. That is a huge reversal in expectations compared to the sixties, which were marked through and through by a "sense of history." The present is no longer a moment of tension between the past and the future but a sort of morass, a perpetual present. As François Hartog says, modern "presentism" has replaced the "historicism" of the previous generations.[10]

Aldo Schiavone, in his remarkable *History and Destiny*, revisits this transformation in his own manner.[11] The technological world abolishes the future, he writes, because it is its own transcendence. Like the game of Go the machine won, the technological world is flat, without critical depth; it does not hit the pause button that allows it time to ponder its own destiny. Writing once offered a bridge between generations, so that everyone to understand who they were relative to others. According to Lévi-Strauss, the societies without history were those that did not make the transition to writing. It is possible that the world we are entering, that of the hypertext and video games, will lead us to lose the critical distance that fosters historical consciousness.

As in the film *The Matrix*, the virtual world is replacing the real world. Power outages are needed to stop "the true" from being "a moment of the false," as Guy Debord said in *The Society of the Spectacle*.

Algorithmic Life

The emancipation of the individual was expected to be the major event of our time. The change that came in the eighties, with the first desktop computers and the Walkman, was interpreted as a new threshold that had been crossed. This trend was later reinforced by the mobile phone, which eliminated the need for a home base (professional or personal) from which to make contact. As Éric Sadin says very well, this was the culmination of the process of liberation begun in the sixties.[12] Originally, "the idea of a new technological environment was supposed to favor individual fulfillment and collective emancipation." This was the hippie dream, the aspiration for universal harmony thanks to universal interconnectedness, the free horizontal circulation of information. In *Being Digital* (1995), Nicholas Negroponte explained that the Internet would "flatten organizations, globalize society, decentralize control, and help harmonize people."[13]

In place of a humanized society that would achieve the emancipatory ideal of May '68 (and the Enlightenment), a digitized society was invented; that's not the same thing. In *Homo deus*, Harari comments ironically on that evolution: "Medieval crusaders believed that God and heaven provided their lives with meaning; modern liberals believe that individual free choices provide life with meaning. They are all equally delusional. We are about to face a flood of extremely useful devices, tools and structures that make no allowance for the free will of individual humans."[14]

The multiplicity of connections silently changes the personalities of Internet users. As Jean Baudrillard says, "The fact that the identity is that of the network, and never of individuals, entails the possibility of concealing oneself there, of disappearing into the impalpable space of the virtual, and thus of no longer being locatable anywhere, even by oneself." From that angle, *Homo digitalis* is a return to certain ancient conceptions of personality. Jean-Pierre Vernant pointed this out: The ancient Greeks lived entirely in "exteriority," before and for other people's eyes. A Greek man was a "he" before being an "I."[15] The digital world in turn creates a social life in which users submit to the constant gaze of others, reverting to a premodern definition of individuality. But the Greeks themselves believed that the social instinct of the citizenry called for a corresponding construction of private spheres. Now everything is tracked: the attention you pay to a TV program, your driving. In the algorithmic life proposed by GAFA (Google, Amazon, FaceBook, Apple) the "private self" is lost and the privacy of the home shattered. The connected house brings a mass of potential suppliers into your private realm. Private life, concludes Sadin, "which assumes that a part of oneself could be shielded from the observation of others, must be entirely revisited."

The NSA and the FBI also have access to the data collected by GAFA. Police surveillance is obviously nothing new. It is the quantitative scope of the phenomenon that brings about a qualitative shift. What is new is that this data is managed by a growing number of players. Ranking for taxi drivers but also for their customers, for the owners and clientele of rooms rented on Airbnb, is acquiring a consuming importance. Universities and researchers are regularly ranked by "independent boards," which, though they try to be neutral, profoundly disrupt the academic world. In order to be included in the Shanghai ranking, for example, universities are impelled to adopt cluster policies designed to make them as large as possible (the flaw in the Shanghai ranking is that it does not correct for the size of the institution).

In China, a very disturbing social ranking system of individuals is being set in place. A "citizen score" will rank social behaviors, whether car accidents, absenteeism, consumption of alcohol, late payments, and "naturally," the remarks individuals make on their blogs. That system became compulsory in 2020.[16] Democratic countries are not safe. Applications that measure lifestyle (sports activities, the number of steps taken daily, and so on) could provide criteria for insurance companies to decide their rates. In the United States, an individual score, FICO, already exists for deciding whether credit ought to be extended. At present, it takes into account only late payments, but nothing prevents it from evolving some day. The response of the former CEO of Google, Eric Schmidt, when asked about the dissemination of data, leaves you speechless: "If you have something that you don't want anyone to know, perhaps you shouldn't be doing it in the first place." [17] Alas, that is a terrible confession about the world according to GAFA: nothing hidden, no respite for the soul.

Addiction is the other major mode of life in the digital world. Netflix is an excellent example of this new process. Series are always constructed in the same way: several parallel stories keep the viewer in suspense; good characters turn bad and vice versa. The series is the great cultural creation of digital society, just as film was for electricity. It illustrates one of the essential driving forces of the digital world: keep people waiting, for an e-mail, a text, a news alert.[18] According to Jacques-Alain Miller, Jacques Lacan's son-in-law and the editor of his seminars, "The general model for everyday life in the twenty-first century is addiction. The 'One' finds enjoyment all alone with drugs, and any activity can become a drug: sports, sex, work, smartphone, Facebook."[19]

In *Civilization and Its Discontents*, Freud remarks that humanity is not programmed for happiness, which is never anything but a transitory state. It is like the sensation a dreamer gets by sticking a leg out from under the blanket when hot and pulling it back in when cold. Harari reminds us that many people do not find satisfaction: The every-growing consumption of drugs is evidence, he writes, of that revolt against the fallibility of human happiness. In artificially creating the addictive need to be plugged in, to have the experience of a Web series and then have to wait for the next episode, the digital world creates the disease it knows how to cure, artificially producing at will the pleasure of the leg you stick out and pull back in.

Like any coherent system, the cyberworld also produces the instruments by which it can be challenged. If Facebook is the tool of a social instinct that aspires to be consensual through the filter of kindness, Twitter is the space for a loss of control, which explains why Donald Trump makes such great use of it. A number of prominent figures had to close their accounts under the avalanche of insults addressed to them. Beneath the visible stratum of self-presentation, another, subterranean, world is created on the Internet, as if by way of compensation. This is the world of aliases and avatars, which liberates tremendous urges and impulses, while keeping the user protected from anonymity. This new subterranean world radically modifies the rules of the social game. On the Internet, "nobody knows you're a dog," as the famous cartoon published in the *New Yorker* has it. Philip Rosedale created the concept of *Second Life*, a universe where a person can act through an avatar. Antonio Casilli's analysis of the case of Japan shows the new reality of the society that emerges when individuals act from behind the veil of anonymity. The 2channel message board (*ni channeru* in Japanese), in which all the actors are concealed behind screen names, has become one of the most visited in the world, with 2.5 million subscribers. It shows a face of Japanese society that is the exact opposite of the one seen in broad daylight (usually modest, respectful of hierarchies). It is one of the most indecent sites in the world: illegal pornography, defamations of private individuals and public figures, and crude profanity are the rule. Millions of faceless users escape to it, at the risk of "losing face."

The paradox of the younger generations born after the advent of social networks is that people have never displayed themselves so much and, at the same time, have never made such widespread use of masks.[20] Fictive identities create the sense that the face we are contemplating on our smartphone screen is no longer truly ours but rather a digital self. The monstrous stands side by side with the ordinary, with nothing in between. As Pauline Escande-Gauquié and Bertrand Naivin write, Kim Kardashian is a Cicciolina 2.0, a caricature of total excess: "an excess of breasts, buttocks, and mouth. She constantly exhibits a borderline body, one falling outside the norms." At the other extreme, emaciated, anorectic bodies are on display, fueling idiotic bets about who can have the skinniest thighs.

For Escande-Gauquié and Naivin, the digital world is that of the unbounded infinite where anything goes and where critical reflection is therefore impossible. Digital culture, presenting itself as heir to an individualist tradition, has constructed a hybrid being of networks and algorithms. Individuals spend more time publicizing an event than experiencing it. People scroll from one conversation to another, from one lover to another, thanks to Tinder and other apps that always offer the same promise, that of living several lives at once, everywhere at the same time. "In giving priority to live interactions," they conclude, "social networks cut short any possibility that the superego and self-control will find expression; they offer every human urge, every drive, the chance to come gushing out." By means of these different artifices, *Homo digitalis* quite simply threatens to "dispossess us of ourselves."

The Life Ahead

We have come full circle. May '68 wanted to break free from industrial society. A new, equally demanding world with its rules, promises, and threats is now being constructed, one in which we must learn to live. It would be just as useless now to reject the Internet as it would have been to spurn electricity in the twentieth century or the railroad in the nineteenth. But digital society must also learn to live with us, individuals composed of flesh and dreams. New regulations must be followed, new social and artistic critiques made, to keep the digital world from swallowing us up entirely in its network of surveillance and addictions.

Regulation of this world entails, in the first place, scrutiny of GAFA. Their size raises the same questions as those that arose with the emergence of American giants such as Standard Oil in the early twentieth century. The antitrust laws passed at the time must be rethought. Antitrust agencies have shown a great deal of indulgence in allowing GAFA not only to capture a growing share of the digital market but also to buy out potential competitors, as Facebook did with Instagram and WhatsApp. We must consider taking away the near monopoly they enjoy. We need, for example, to create public databanks on important subjects, such as Alzheimer's, and oblige public or private organizations to share the information they hold to advance major causes in the general interest. Public institutions, hospitals and schools especially, must have the means available to reflect independently about the solutions offered by artificial intelligence. Coordinated care networks, for example, linking hospitals and outpatient care, must be fostered, and there is no reason why public hospitals cannot take a leadership role in that process. Similarly, it is possible to imagine digital assistance for students who are struggling, programs designed by the national education system itself with the support of the teaching staff.

The disappearance of privacy on social networks is another crucial matter that should be subject to specific regulations. The Internet created this strange world, where private data can be sold to all comers, even as the anonymity of the authors of hate-filled screeds is protected. A digital habeas corpus has become indispensable, like the one English law introduced in the Middle Ages to protect individuals from the risks of arbitrary detention. This need became particularly obvious with the Cambridge Analytica scandal. That heinous company, which has since gone bankrupt, stole the information of several tens of millions of Facebook users to promote presidential candidate Trump, allowing his team to scientifically target undecided voters. When we recall that the 2016 election hinged on a few tens of thousands of voters in the swing states, it is not an overstatement to say that Trump's victory over Clinton may have been the result of that wrongdoing.

It is clear that self-regulation will not suffice, even though GAFA members all portray themselves as paragons of virtue. The European Commission took the initiative, laying the foundations for a right to protect individual data, a directive that went into effect in May 2018. Google anticipated it by refraining from data-mining the e-mails written with its service. By expanding French regulations and the legal precedents of the National Commission on Computing and Civil Liberties, the European Commission is promoting new protections, such as the right to be forgotten, which prohibits accusations for which a person has been cleared from appearing in Internet searches. The imperative of transparency regarding the algorithms used by public and private groups will also assume growing importance, as their power in managing people's lives increases, whether in credit decisions or in admissions to universities. Public authorities must be accountable for the algorithms they use, and the same rule must be applied in the private sector. All of that requires effective oversight authorities and watchdogs.

The digital world as a whole most pose questions about itself on the scale of its responsibilities. Reflections about a new system of social regulation is one of the priorities, at a time when a growing number of jobs are being Uberized. In dismantling Fordist society, the new society has destroyed the de facto solidarity that existed between the cleaning woman and the engineer, in the old days when they worked for the same employer. A service society, where workers are employed in workshop-type environments, has a great deal of trouble rebuilding such connections. At stake in the new professional social security, as it is called, is how to design a model that will guarantee new protections against the risks of everyday life in the fragmented contemporary world.

One of the institutions that has suffered most from the dismantlement of the old model is trade unionism. Some would like to consider it no longer necessary. During the nineties, thanks to the return of full employment, American society showed that a service society could put to good use a revived trade unionism. Philippe Askenazy has analyzed how the incidence of work accidents, which skyrocketed in the eighties, finally fell thanks to the actions of a new union leadership. The "Justice for Janitors" campaign, for example, succeeded in unionizing thousands of employees in the building maintenance sector, improving their working conditions. It met its objectives: The number of work accidents fell precipitously. Trade unionism is as fundamental to the world of work as representative democracy is to political life: it gives workers a collective means of expression. The regions of the world where trade unionism has remained strong, in the Scandinavian countries especially, are also those where daring social experiments have been possible, whether the Wassenaar Arrangement in the Netherlands or Danish *flexicurity*. Unions' actions are becoming all the more crucial in that the employer may be far removed from the real world where people work, or may even be a digital platform with which it is difficult to take issue.

Other ideas aimed at giving individuals greater security have also made their appearance in recent debates. The idea of a universal basic income was one of the innovative aspects of the French presidential campaign in 2017. The catastrophic showing of the candidate who promoted it—Benoît Hamon received only 6.4 percent of the vote—indicates that there is still a long way to go before it makes inroads in political life. Its adversaries have denounced it as an eschewal of work, a right to laziness. But there is no reason to associate the universal basic income with the end of work. In fact, Philippe Van Parijs, one of its principal theorists, places them in radical opposition.[21] The reduction of work time, he explains, was the great idea of the twentieth century. Universal basic income is the great idea of the twenty-first. It is an instrument that should allow us, not to work less, but to resist the blackmail endured by those who must accept substandard jobs in the gig economy to survive. Thomas Paine, one of its first defenders, saw the universal basic income as a way to correct inequality between those who receive inheritances and everyone else.[22] No one has ever claimed that inheriting dissuades people from working. The aim of the basic universal income is to provide a soothing answer to the question that haunts society: Where is human labor headed? In an approach inspired by Amartya Sen, it can be defined as the conquest of a freedom that allows one to turn down ignominious jobs, to construct a destiny worthy of one's aspirations, whether as an artist or a peasant.

We must also fortify a new artistic critique that challenges digital society's way of keeping us under house arrest behind its screens. Our era makes it more necessary than ever to cultivate the art of interruption or deferral. Days without Facebook have proven to be the source of a surplus of well-being, like the Sabbath in ancient times. It has become almost impossible to have a conversation with someone without being interrupted by a text or call that must be answered immediately. A recivilizing process in interpersonal relationships has become indispensable. As David Remnick, editor of the *New Yorker*, has said, we must ponder our own digital obsessions, their effect on our attention to others, our critical sense. "The triumphs and wonders of the Internet age have been obvious," he writes, but the time for a "moral reckoning" has come.

A new digital citizenship will require that the education of children and adolescents be adapted to the challenges they will face. Both Sadin and Tisseron point out the importance of teaching young people how to code, not so they will necessarily become computer scientists, but so they will learn that robots are governed by algorithms, and that algorithms are made and unmade by humans. That is the best way to keep from endowing robots with supernatural qualities that would paralyze humans in the face of their demands. The culture of the written word, of the book, is the other indispensable pillar that must be protected. This consists less of getting students to produce flawless spelling tests than of fostering a love of reading. French young people, whose OECD ranking is falling, struggle much more to understand the meaning of a text than to read it in the narrow sense. In Roberto Casilli's tongue-in-cheek analysis the book is a contract between the author and the reader.[23] Authors pledge to leave readers free to interpret a book as they will, while readers grant a monopoly on their attention to authors, at least for a certain time. If writers must compete with the thousand temptations of the iPad, they will ultimately prefer to play on the emotions rather than construct an argument. That does not mean that the e-book is a bad thing, even if authors like Milan Kundera are fiercely opposed to it. But we must create a blockade, deactivate the options, turn off the Internet connection, to give the author a chance— especially, of course, in the case of books for young people.

On the critical climate change issue, the digital world may be a tool to fight against global warming. Certainly, the new technologies can optimize old industrial society, can more effectively mitigate the damage, congestion, trash, and pollution of all kinds. The artificial intelligence used by General Electric, for example, can reduce by nearly 40 percent the demand for electricity. The promise of "smart cities" lies entirely in reducing the consumption of energy to the absolute minimum, thanks to the optimization of existing management processes. The problem is that this minimum still remains far too high. The digital world itself emits an enormous quantity of carbon dioxide. Computers consume huge amounts of energy. Facebook has therefore moved some of its data centers to Norway, about sixty miles from the Arctic Circle, to reduce the heat emitted by its computers. A comparison with the human brain illustrates clearly digital society's voracious appetite for energy. When it simulates the human brain's 100 billion neurons, the most powerful computer in the world, Sequoia, consumes 12 gigawatts, that is, the equivalent of the power of the giant Itaipu Dam on the border of Brazil and Paraguay. Human beings, by comparison, are a model of environmental frugality: They consume less than 20 watts. The world of the new technologies still has a long way to go before it converges with the ecological imperative of a more abstemious world.

The ideal of a postmaterialist society that emerged in the sixties receded with the blow of the financial crisis and the insecurity it caused. The problem is that "crises" have become a new norm. Universal basic income is one instrument that might allow a response to that need for security, providing an intermediate space between the urgent need to survive and the desire to live. But we must go further. The remarks André Gorz made in the seventies in *Farewell to the Proletariat* are still wholly relevant: "Capitalism removed the desire or the ability to reflect on the 'real' needs of every individual, to debate with others the best means to satisfy them, and to define in full autonomy the alternatives that might be explored."[24]

That must be the role of a new artistic critique: to allow everyone to retain a rebellious awareness of their "true" needs.

Conclusion

FROM DYLAN TO DEEPMIND

CAPITALISM IS THE RESULT of a Faustian bargain, a grand deal, as Yuval Noah Harari puts it, between science and money. "For thousands of years," he recalls with humor, "priests, rabbis and muftis explained that humans cannot overcome famine, plague and war by their own efforts. Then along came bankers, investors and industrialists, and within 200 years managed to do exactly that."[1] For the first time in human history, the number of suicides exceeds the number of deaths on the battlefield. People are more likely to die of obesity than of starvation. Prosperity has won out over poverty. But "history does not tolerate a vacuum," Harari adds, and "if incidences of famine, plague and war are decreasing, something is bound to take their place on the human agenda." After a period of hesitations and faltering steps in the seventies, the contract between technology and capitalism has been renewed, with the promise that it will be further extended.

It is worth observing that the uncontrollable thirst for growth in modern societies has still not been satisfied. The

issue of purchasing power continues to preoccupy most countries, especially France, even though it is twice as wealthy now as
it was in 1968. As Hirschman emphasized in the mid-seventies,
wealth is always relative. When millionaires are asked what
level of wealth they would need to be truly comfortable, they
all respond the same way, whatever level they have already
achieved: twice what they already possess. Economists who
specialize in happiness have dissected this paradox, which
is attributed to the great economist Richard Easterlin. An
increase in income allows individuals to think they are rising above their condition. But the sense that they are rich
quickly dissolves when they compare themselves to others.
If others also get rich, I discover that my relative position has
not improved or even, if inequalities have increased, that it has
deteriorated.

Democratic society is a powerful stimulus of that "mimetic
rivalry," to use René Girard's expression. No comparison is
out of bounds: "If he has it, why can't I?" could be one of its
slogans. In that respect, economic growth has proved to be a
remarkable means of social pacification. Workers who know
that, in ten or fifteen years, they will have access to the same
basket of goods as their employer are reassured about their
social status. "He has a car, soon I'll have one too! We live in the
same world." Harking back to his early memories, Jean-Pierre
Le Goff recounts that "the arrival of the washing machine was
an event, not only because it liberated my mother and sister
from 'laundry duty' but also because this 'machine that washes
the laundry all by itself' looked like a first-rate technological
invention. . . . Television and the 'passenger vehicle' held a special place. . . . Where [they] had previously been considered a
luxury reserved for the wealthy . . . [they] were now portrayed
as items essential for the enjoyment of weekends and vaca-
tions, time away from work."[2]

Despite its successes, industrial society ultimately grew tiresome. In the sixties, young people shouted themselves hoarse trying to bring down its paternalist order, its Taylorist manias. And, in an unexpected miracle, the order actually collapsed. The causes of its fall had nothing to do with May '68. They were economic: The gains in productivity that were key to the success of the Glorious Thirty came to an end. The promise of "work and you'll get a raise" faded away. With the crisis of the seventies, capitalism "went on to other things." It dismantled the factories, sent home the workers who had populated them, and proceeded full speed to look for new sources of growth.

The sociologist Ronald Inglehart argues that, in its time, industrial society replaced feudal society, even while preserving its verticality. Engineers replaced priests, but the world of production continued to rely on a hierarchical order that was just as rigid as the one established between the lord and his vassal. It is possible that digital society swept away that distant heritage, substituting for it a new social imaginary. The counterculture of the sixties provided the mold. In adopting the "rhizomatic" ideal of horizontality and even of services free of charge, digital society created a new system in which "everything is connected." Everyone must now be online, at home and at the office. Obedience, which had been the mark of the old world of production, has been replaced by an imperative for creativity that proves to be just as demanding.

The digital revolution brought down the old world by causing two radical breaks, in production and in consumption. In the first place, lower communications costs made possible a tremendous reengineering of firms, as work was contracted beyond the traditional boundaries of businesses and national borders. That reorganization was guided by a single principle, drawn directly from those Adam Smith had once laid out: As much as possible, let the market cut production costs. By outsourcing everything that could be outsourced—workers and suppliers—this reengineering destroyed the implicit solidarity that the old industrial world, hierarchical but interdependent, had ultimately built.

The resurgence of that "low-cost" capitalism has caused a new pauperization of the working classes. The surprise, which stunned observers and the political class, is that this shift sowed the seeds of a new populism and reinvented the Far Right. Its comeback should not have been a surprise, however. It is very similar to the situation already observed in the thirties. The dissolution of industrial society caused a social disconnect that hit the working classes full force, *disconnected*—in all senses of the term—as they were from the rest of the world. In the eyes of Trump or Marine Le Pen voters, the central question is not redistribution or even exploitation, but rather the fear of social exclusion, the loss of one's relationship to others.

The new technologies have also had an effect on consumption. In the twentieth century, by promising everyone cars and nylon stockings, capitalism broadened its social base.[3] By offering the masses what was previously "a luxury reserved for the wealthy," capitalism won them over. What does it now offer to reignite desires? According to the transhumanists, nothing less is at issue than to elevate human beings to the level of the gods, hoist them above their biological humanity and give them access to immortality. More prosaically, in a service economy, humans are the new product, that are to be educated, connected, repaired, entertained. The digital world "industrializes" the service economy, creating a hybrid being of flesh and algorithms.

What must now be reinvented is a new critique—social and artistic—that opens a breach in the way our lives are being reconfigured by the new imperative for growth. Will we know how to extract what is best from digital society, without having to renounce to our humanistic values? As Aldo Schiavone says (in *History and Destiny*), "We need a new humanism that will construct an integrated and all-encompassing rationality that is equal to our responsibilities. We cannot leave technology, and the network of powers that pervades it, to decide without mediation the ways of life available to us. It appears increasingly necessary to find an equilibrium point that, even while integrating the connection between technology and the market, stands on the outside. This would allow it to elaborate what will make its appearance as a common good."

There you have a magnificent program that will be, undoubtedly, the next half-century's task.

NOTES

Preface to the English Edition

1. Jean Fourastié, *Le grand espoir du 20ième siècle* (Paris, PUF, 1948).
2. William Baumol and William Bowen, *Performing Arts, The Economic Dilemma* (New York: Twentieth Century Fund, 1968).

Introduction

1. Karl Marx, *The Eighteenth Brumaire of Louis Bonaparte*, 1852.
2. Edmund Burke, *Reflections on the French Revolution*, 1790.
3. Christopher Lasch, *The True and Only Heaven: Progress and Its Critics*, (New York: Norton, 1991).
4. In *L'idée d'humanité*, Robert Legros would say that modern human beings constantly oscillate between a desire for "uprooting," a desire lauded by the philosophy of the Enlightenment in the eighteenth century, and a contradictory need for "rootedness," expressed by the romanticism of the nineteenth century. (Robert Legros, *L'idée d'humanité*, Grasset, 1990).
5. Jean Fourastié, *Le grand espoir du 20ième siècle* (Paris: PUF, 1948).

Chapter 1: Modern Mythologies

1. Cornelius Castoriadis wrote: "The interpretation of May '68 in terms of the preparation for (or acceleration of) contemporary individualism is one of the most extreme attempts I know of to rewrite [history] against all verisimilitude. What is forgotten are the weeks of fraternization and active solidarity, when you spoke to anyone in life, without being afraid of looking like a madman, when every driver stopped to give you a lift. So their truth was hedonistic egoism?" Edgar Morin, Claude Lefort, and Cornelius Castoriadis, *Mai 68. La brèche: suivie de Vingt ans après* (Paris: Fayard, 1988).
2. Jean-Pierre Le Goff, *La France d'hier* (Paris: Stock, 2018).
3. On all these points, see Benjamin Coriat, *L'atelier et le chronomètre* (Paris: Christian Bourgois, 1994).
4. Roland Barthes, *Mythologies*, trans. Annette Lavers (New York: Hill and Wang, 1972).
5. Jean Baudrillard, *La société de consommation* (Paris : Gallimard, 1970).
6. Albert Hirschman, *Shifting Involvements, Private Interest and Public Action* (Princeton, Princeton University Press, 1982).

7. As Henri Weber recalls in his memoirs, the idea at the time was exactly the opposite. It was thought that the crisis of capitalism would make for the success of the Far Left. Henri Weber, *Rebelle jeunesse* (Paris: Stock, 2018).

8. Patrick Rotman, *Mai 68 raconté à ceux qui ne l'ont pas vécu*, (Paris: Le Seuil, 2008).

9. The Cuban revolution against the United States aroused the passions of young students. Photos of Che, the romantic figure par excellence, staring out toward the horizon, were everywhere.

10. He would die ten years later, on December 24, 1979.

11. One of the (many) paradoxes of that period was that the peace talks began in Paris on May 10, 1968.

12. The old so defined are now more numerous than the young (under twenty).

13. In an article published on June 22nd, 1963 in *Le Monde*.

14. Le Goff, *La France*.

15. Pierre Viansson-Ponté, "Quand la France s'ennuie . . .", *Le Monde*, 15 mars 1968.

16. Henri Mendras, *La seconde revolution française*, (Paris: Gallimard, 1988).

17. Michelle Perrot, Preface to *Filles de Mai. 68 mon mai à moi. Mémoires de femmes* (Lormont: Le Bord de l'eau, 2004).

18. Ludivine Bantigny, *1968. De grands soirs en petits matins* (Paris: Le Seuil, 2018).

19. Jean-Pierre Le Goff, Interview, *Le Monde*, March 8, 2018.

20. Jean-Pierre Le Goff, *Mai 68, l'héritage impossible* (Paris: La Découverte, 1998).

21. Christian Baudelot, Roger Establet, "Une jeunesse en panne d'avenir." In *Une jeunesse difficile*, ed. Daniel Cohen (CEPREMAP, 2006).

22. Daniel Cohen, ed., *Une jeunesse difficile* (Éditions rue d'Ulm, 2007).

23. Internationale Situationniste, "De la misère en milieu étudiant," 1966.

24. Translations of the book were also a resounding success, proof of the concomitance of that question in all the industrialized countries. Three hundred thousand copies were printed and distributed in eight languages.

25. Pierre Bourdieu, *Interventions, 1961–2001. Science sociale et action politique* (Marseille : Agone, 2002).

26. Louis Chauvel, *Le destin des générations. Structure sociale et cohortes en France au XXe siècle* (PUF, 2002).

27. Eric Maurin, *Vive la Révolution* (La République des Idées, 2005).

28. Luc Boltanski and Ève Chiapello, *Le nouvel esprit du capitalisme* (Paris: Gallimard, 1999).

29. Guy Debord, *La société du spectacle* (Paris: Buchet-Chastel, 1967).

30. Louis Althusser, *L'établi* (Paris: Editions de Minuit, 1978).

31. Virginie Linhart, *Le jour où mon père s'est tu*, (Paris : Le Seuil, 2008).

32. Edgar Morin would link them in the following manner: "The disappointed Trotskyist can turn into a hippie or neo-hippie, and vice versa."

33. That duality of capitalism is also found in sociological analyses. Capitalism stems from a Protestant ethic, an asceticism, according to Max Weber, and

from an appetite for wealth according to Werner Sombard. For Bell, these analyses express the duality between the bourgeois spirit of "calculation and order" and the Faustian desire for a world without limits.

34. Herbert Marcuse, *One-Dimensional Man* (Boston: Beacon Press, 1964).

35. Herbert Marcuse, *Eros and Civilization* (Boston: Beacon Press, 1955).

36. Wilhelm Reich, *The Sexual Revolution* (New York: Farrar, Straus and Girous, 1974).

37. For Freud, though civilization did require a higher level of repression, it compensated the human soul with a better understanding of itself.

38. Vincent Descombes, *Le même et l'autre* (Paris, Les Éditions de Minuit, 1979).

39. "Desire is not the appetite for satisfaction, nor the demand for love, but the difference that results from the subtraction of the former from the latter." Jacques Lacan "La signification du phallus," in *Écrits* (Paris: Seuil, 1966).

40. In *La volonté de savoir*, the first volume of *Histoire de la sexualité*, Michel Foucault would criticize in turn "the repressive hypothesis" at the foundation of Marcuse's analysis. Michel Foucault, *Histoire de la sexualité* (Paris : Gallimard, 2013.)

41. Claude Lévi-Strauss *La Pensée sauvage* (Paris: Plon, 1962).

42. Lévi-Strauss *La Pensée sauvage*.

43. Perhaps, added Lévi-Straus, "that golden age of historical consciousness is already past; and the fact that one can at least conceive of that eventuality proves that it is only a contingent situation."

44. *Les mots et les choses* (Paris, Gallimard, 1966).

45. Linhart, *Le jour*.

46. Serge Audier, *La pensée anti-68* (La Decouverte, 2008).

Chapter 2: Lost Illusions (1/3)

1. Paul Krugman, *The Age of Diminished Expectations* (Cambridge: MIT Press, 1990).

2. Robert Gordon, *The Rise and Fall of American Growth* (Princeton University Press, 2017).

3. John Kenneth Galbraith, *The Affluent Society* (1958, Houghton Miffin).

4. Lionel Fontagné, Hervé Boulhol, "Deindustrialisation and the Fear of Relocations in the Industry," CEPII Working Paper No 2006–07 (CEPII 2006).

5. Robert Rowthorn, Ramana Ramaswamy, "Growth, Trade, and Deindustrialization," IMF Working Paper 60, February 15, 2006.

6. Andre Gorz, *Farewell to the Working Class* (Paris: Editions Galilée,1980).

7. Marx developed a different argument in the *Grundrisse*, however, a text less well known than *Das Kapital*. As Gorz would point out, Marx believed that "the polytechnical" worker, driven to improve and automate the technologies of production, would abolish unskilled labor and leave only high-level technical workers who had an overall view of the technico-economic processes and were able to manage production internally."

8. Bernard Lacroix, *L'utopie communautaire. Mai 68, histoire sociale d'une révolte* (Paris: PUF, 1982).

9. Roger-Pol Droit and Antoine Gallien, *La chasse au bonheur. Les nouvelles communautés en France* (Paris: Calmann-Lévy, 1972).

10. Virginie Linhart, *La vie après* (Paris: Le Seuil, 2012).

11. La Croix, *L'utopie*.

12. In addition, communes rarely have a balanced sex ratio. "Usually, the number of men greatly surpasses the number of women, resulting in competition, squabbles, quarrels, and rivalries."

13. Bruno Bettelheim, *The Children of the Dream*, (London: Paladin, 1979).

14. According to a woman quoted by Bettelheim: "Let's face it, the kibbutz wasn't built for children, but to make us free." Bettelheim analyzes in minute detail the way guilt was warded off. The women he met constantly repeated to him that the kibbutz is the best environment possible for children.

15. Erving Goffman, *The Presentation of the Self in Everyday Life* (New York: Doubleday, 1959).

16. La Croix, *L'utopie*.

17. Nonetheless, the Christian Democratic Party would continue to win elections at the expense of the Communist Party, making unnecessary the maneuvers of Moro and Berlinguer, general secretary of the Communist Party, to prepare the way for a large coalition.

18. Leonardo Sciascia, *La scomparsa di Majorana* (Turin: Einaudi, 1975).

19. Sciascia, *La Scomparsa*.

20. Henri Weber, *Vingt ans après, que reste-t-il de mai 68?* (Paris: Le Seuil, 1988).

21. Rotman, *Mai 68*.

22. Steven Pinker, *The Better Angels of Our Nature* (New York: Viking Books, 2011).

23. Robert Muchembled, *Une histoire de la violence* (Paris: Le Seuil, 2010).

24. Chicago, *Chicago Transit Authority* (New York: Columbia, 1969).

25. Jerry Rubin, *Do It* (Paris: Seuil, 1973).

26. Cas Wouters, *Informalization, Manners and Emotion since 1890* (Los Angeles: Sage, 2007).

27. The increase in the number of young people is also mentioned as a factor, the young being on average more violent than adults. The effects of this factor were secondary, however. If the rate of criminality among the young had remained unchanged, the increase would have been modest, 13 percent.

Chapter 3: The Conservative Revolution

1. Guy Sorman, *La révolution conservatrice américaine* (Paris: Fayard, 1983).

2. Thomas Sowell, *Race and economics* (David Mac Kay Publications, 1975).

3. In *The Rhetoric of Reaction*, Albert Hirschman explains that it is characteristic of conservative discourse to denounce the perverse effect of measures

intended to fight inequality. Albert Hirschman, *The Rhetoric of Reaction* (Cambridge: Belknap Press, 1991).

4. George Gilder, *Visible Man: A True Story of Post-Racist America* (San Francisco: ICS Press, 1995).

5. Charles Murray, *The Bell Curve: Intelligence and Class Structure in American Life* (New York: Free Press, 1994).

6. Orley Ashenfelter, "Schooling, Intelligence, and Income in America: Cracks in the Bell Curve," *American Economic Review* (December 1994).

7. Eva Illouz, in *Die große Regression. Eine internationale Debatte über die geistige Situation der Zeit*, ed. Heinrich Geiselberger (Berlin: Suhrkamp Verlag, 2017).

8. Daniel Linderberg, *Le procès des Lumières* (Paris: Le Seuil, 2009).

9. Guy Sorman, *La révolution*.

10. Joseph de Maistre, *Considérations sur la France* (1796).

11. Christopher Lasch, *The True and Only Heaven*.

12. Lasch adds: "My own faith in the explanatory power of the old ideologies began to waver in the mid-seventies, when my study of the family led me to question the left's program of sexual liberation, careers for women, and professional child care."

13. Allan Bloom, *The Closing of the American Mind* (New York: Simon and Schuster, 1987).

14. In a democracy, as de Tocqueville said, tradition is nothing more than information. With the explosion of information, tradition has become superfluous. One of the corollaries is the loss of a penchant for reading, which Allan Bloom observed in the late 1960s: "The notion of books as companions is foreign to them."

15. Burke, *Reflections*.

16. Stephen D. Oliner and Daniel E. Sichel, "The Resurgence of Growth in the Late 1990s: Is Information Technology the Story?" *Journal of Economic Perspectives* 14, no. 1 (Autumn 2000). For the French data, see Gilberte Cette, Simon Corde, and Rémy Lecat, "Rupture de tendance de la productivité en France. Quel impact de la crise?" *Économie et Statistique* (2017).

17. Nikolai Kondratiev, *The Long Wave Cycle*, (New York: Richardson and Snyder, 1984).

18. Betsey Stevenson and Justin Wolfers, "Marriage and Divorce: Changes and Their Driving Forces," *Journal of Economic Perspectives* 21, no. 2 (2007).

19. Benjamin Friedman, *The Moral Consequences of Economic Growth* (Penguin, 1985).

20. Facundo Alvaredo, Lucas Chancel, Thomas Piketty, Emmanuel Saez, and Gabriel Zucman, eds., *World Inequality Report, 2018* (Cambridge: Belknap Press, 2018).

21. Richard Freeman, with Erling Barth, Alex Bryson, and C. James Davis, "It's Where You Work: Increases in Earnings Dispersion across Establishments and Individuals in the U.S.," *NBER* 20447 (2014).

22. Philippe Askenazy, *La croissance moderne. Organisations innovantes du travail* (Paris: Economica, 2002).

23. Alain Ehrenberg, *Le culte de la performance* (Paris: Calmann-Lévy, 1991).

24. Luc Boltanski, Éve Chiapallo, *Le nouvel esprit du capitalisme*, (Paris: Gallimard, 1999).

25. Philippe Askenazy, *Les désordres du travail. Enquête sur le nouveau productivisme* (Le Seuil, 2004).

Chapter 4: The Proletariat's Farewell

1. Emmanuel Levinas, *Les imprévus de l'histoire* (Paris: Fata Morgana, 1992).

2. Peter Sloterdijk, *Rage and Time* (New York: Columbia University Press, 2006).

3. Max Schuler, *L'homme du ressentiment* (Paris: Gallimard, 1970).

4. Rudiger Dornbusch and Sebastian Edwards, *The Macroeconomics of Populism in Latin America* (Cambridge: NBER, 1991).

5. Dominique Reynié, *Les nouveaux populismes* (Paris: Pluriel, 2013).

6. Sixty-seven percent of "whites without a college education" voted for Trump.

7. Trump received 62 percent of the vote among Americans who live in rural areas or small towns. By contrast, Hillary Clinton had her best showing (59 percent) in cities of more than fifty-eight thousand. The role of low population density and low educational level is the major takeaway of the vote for Trump and for the National Front. The red states have a geographical area four times larger than that of the blue states.

8. Thomas Frank, *What's the Matter with Kansas?* (New York: Metropolitan, 2005).

9. Brice Teinturier, *Plus rien à faire, plus rien à foutre* (Paris: Robert Laffont, 2017).

10. Michael Sandel, *Tyranny of Merit* (New York: Farrar, Straus and Giroux, 2020).

11. Ian Kershaw, *To Hell and Back, Europe 1914–1949* (Viking, 2015).

12. Jonathan Freeland, "Eugenics: The Skeleton That Rattles Loudest in the Left's Closet," *The Guardian*, February 17, 2012.

13. The book comprises three parts: *Anti-Semitism*, *Imperialism*, and *Totalitarianism*. Pierre Bouretz's introduction to the French edition, titled "Between Passion and Reason," outlines perfectly what is primarily at stake in the book: to understand how the West, whose rise sociologists from Max Weber to Norbert Elias interpreted as an effort to rationalize the passions, could be overwhelmed by the Nazi impulse.

14. Hannah Arendt, *Men in Dark Times* (Stellar, 2014).

15. Yann Algan, Elizabeth Beasley, Daniel Cohen, and Martial Foucault, "The Rise of Populism and the Collapse of the Left-Right Paradigm," working paper (CEPREMAP, 2018).

16. As Hervé Le Bras indicates, 48 percent of workers from Champagne-Ardenne (in the northeast) vote for the National Front, but only 15 percent of those in the Midi-Pyrénées region. Such discrepancies reveal that the category

of "workers" is insufficient for grasping the nature of the party's vote. The CEVIPOF survey shows, however, that downward mobility in relation to one's father's profession is a factor that partly explains the Le Pen vote. At issue here is individual resentment. Hervé Le Bras, *Le Pari du FN* (Paris: Autrement, 2015).

17. The CEVIPOF survey allows us to measure subjective variables, such as dissatisfaction or well-being. The two candidates for whom subjective well-being plays the most important role in explaining the vote are Le Pen (negative effect) and Macron (positive effect).

18. Robert Castel, *L'insécurité sociale* (Paris: Seuil, 2003).

19. Hervé Le Bras, *Le pari du FN* (Paris: Editions Autrement, 2015).

20. Serge Paugam, *Vivre ensemble dans un monde incertain* (La tour d'Aigues: Éditions de l'Aube, 2015).

21. Serge Paugam also adds an incisive remark: "Paradoxically with respect to the idea that they disrupt the social order, communities of drug traffickers and other criminals are also searching for an alternative mode of social integration." Furthermore, affiliation (often imaginary) with a Muslim religious community serves as compensation for populations facing the same difficulties of social integration as their enemies, the National Front voters.

22. Gilles Deleuze and Félix Guattari, *L'Anti-Oedipe* (Paris: Éditions de Minuit, 1972).

Chapter 5: Immigration Phobia

1. Jacques Lacan, *Télévision* (Paris: Seuil, 1974).

2. Conversely, Mélenchon voters, who are just as "antisystem" as Le Pen voters, demonstrate very strong trust in others. See Yann Algan, Elizabeth Beasley, Daniel Cohen, and Martial Foucault, *The Rise of Populism* (London: Centre for Economic Policy Research, 2018).

3. Lant Pritchett, *Let Their People Come* (Washington, D.C.: Center for Global Development, 2006).

4. Pritchett, *Let Their People Come*.

5. David Card, "The impact of the Mariel Boat Lift on the Miami Labor Market", *Industrial and Labor Relations Review* 43 (January 1990).

6. George J. Borjas, "The wage impact of the Marielitos", *Industrial and Labor Relations Review* 70, no. 5 (August 2019).

7. See Hillel Rapoport, *Repenser l'immigration en France. Un point de vue économique* (Paris: Éditions rue d'Ulm, 2018); and El Mouhoub Mouhoud, *L'immigration en France* (Paris: Fayard, 2017).

8. René Girard, *Mensonge romantique et vérité Romanesque* (Paris: Grasset, 1961).

9. Ian Buruma, *Murder in Amsterdam: Liberal Europe, Islam, and the Limits of Tolerance* (New York: Penguin, 2006).

10. Shalom Schwartz, "An overview of the Schwartz Theory of Basic Values," *Online Readings in Psychology and Culture,* (Hebrew University of Jerusalem, 2012).

11. Schwartz proposes a taxonomy of "values" arranged into four quadrants. The first quadrant of affects has to do with autonomy, "self-direction": all human beings are motivated by the need to achieve mastery of their fate, if only in their minds. The second quadrant is linked to hedonism: human beings seek pleasure and flee suffering. The third quadrant concerns the will to power, the desire to succeed in imposing one's will on others. The last quadrant is that of self-transcendence: justice, kindness.

12. That was also the driving force behind the alliance established in May 2018 between the League and the Five Stars Movement in Italy.

13. Girard, *Mensonge.*

14. Olivier Roy, *Le djihad et la mort* (Paris: Seuil, 2016).

15. Farhad Khosrokhavar, *Le nouveau jihad en Occident* (Paris: Robert Laffont, 2018).

16. Cas Wooters, *Informalization: Manners and Emotions since 1890* (Los Angeles: Sage, 2007).

17. Benyamina and Samitier do not hesitate to speak of a major public health crisis. Amine Benyamina and Marie-Pierre Samitier, *Comment l'alcool détruit la jeunesse. La responsabilité des lobbies et des politiques* (Paris: Albin Michel, 2017).

18. Fabrice Étilé, *Usage des drogues et dépendances*, Thesis, Paris I.

19. Françoise Dolto, *Championing the Cause of Adolescents* (Paris, Robert Laffont, 1988).

20. Alan Kruger, *What Makes a Terrorist: Economics and the Roots of Terrorism* (Princeton: Princeton University Press, 2007).

21. Jean Twenge, *iGen: Why Today's Super-Connected Kids Are Growing Up Less Rebellious, More Tolerant, Less Happy—and Completely Unprepared for Adulthood* (New York: Simon and Schuster, 2017).

22. Quoted by Pauline Escande-Gauquié and Bertrand Naivin in *Monstres 2.0. L'autre visage des réseaux sociaux* (Paris: Éditions François Bourin, 2018).

Chapter 6: The Great Hope of the Twenty-First Century

1. Manuel Castells, Gustavo Cardoso, Paul H. Nitz, *The Network society, From knowledge to Policy,* (Washington, D.C.: Johns Hopkins University, 2006).

2. François Caron, *Le résistible déclin des sociétés industrielles* (Paris: Perrin, 1985).

3. Fourastié, *Le grand espoir.*

4. A firm that enjoys increasing economies of scale can benefit from a cumulative phenomenon: As it develops, it can recoup its costs more easily, which makes it more profitable than small firms, even if they are a priori more efficient. The ascent of GAFA (Google, Amazon, Facebook, and Apple) perfectly illustrates this mechanism.

5. Serge Tisseron, *Le jour où mon robot m'aimera* (Paris: Albin Michel, 2017).

6. Unix is a computer operating system developed by Bell Laboratories. The FCC, which investigated their monopoly, obliged them to place it in the public domain. It was academics who would pursue that development.

7. Thanks to Professor Benabid's team in Grenoble.

8. Contrary to legend, Einstein's brain is not overly large: it weighs only 1.23 kg, compared to an average of 1.4–1.5 kg.

9. Yuval Noah Harari, *Homo Deus* (London: Harvill Secker 2016).

10. Ray Kurzweil, *The Singularity is Near* (Harmondsworth: Penguin, 2005).

11. Hans Moravec, *Mind Children: The Future of Robot and Human Intelligence* (Cambridge, MA: Harvard University Press, 1988).

12. Mark Tegmark, *Life 3.0* (Allen Lane, 2017).

13. Over the last fifty years, the cost of information has dropped so much that, if the same reduction were applied to the city of New York, it would cost only 10 cents, one 10,000 billionth its real worth at present. The cost of calculating falls by a factor of 2 every eighteen months, that is, as Tegmark explains, by a factor of a trillion (10^{18}) since the birth of his grandmother.

14. Danièle Tritsch and Jean Mariani, *Ça va pas la tête?* (Paris: Belin, 2018).

15. Granted, there are stem cells that, after dividing, produce new neurons. But that is an insignificant exception: It is said that seven hundred neurons emerge in the region of the two hippocampi, which is to say, 0.01 percent of the neural population of the area concerned.

16. Francis Wolff, *Trois utopies contemporaines* (Paris: Fayard, 2017).

17. For a machine to think like us, it would have to perceive pain and pleasure. A human being's brain activity is very dependent on its connections to the sense organs (eyes, ears) and to the body parts governing action (walking, gesturing). The intestine is innervated by 200 million neurons: In *Gut: The Inside Story of Our Most Underrated Organ*, Jill Enders and Giulia Enders call it a second brain (Vancouver: Greystone, 2015).

18. Karel Čapek, *R.U.R.* (Prague: Aventinum, 1920).

19. Richard Freeman, "Who Owns the Robots Rules the World" (IZA World of Labor, May 2014).

20. Cited by Mariani and Tritsch, *Ça va pa.*

21. Alfred Sauvy, *La Machine et le Chômage* (Paris: Dunod, 1980).

22. Robert Gordon's dazzling book *The Rise and Fall of American Growth* documents the fall of growth in the advanced countries. Over the decades since the mid-1970s, growth has fallen on average in Europe from 3 percent to 2 percent to 1 percent. For Gordon, it is industrial growth, especially from electricity and the internal combustion engine, that was the exception.

23. Robert Reich, *The Work of Nations* (New York: Vintage, 1992).

24. David H. Autor and David Dorn, "The Growth of Low Skill Service Jobs and the Polarization of the US Labor Market," *American Economic Review* 103, no. 5 (2013). Job polarization designates more generally the disappearance of mid-level jobs in service, management, and industry.

25. Erik Brynjolfsson, Andrew McAfee, Michael Sorell and Feng Zhu, "Scale without Mass," Harvard Business School Technology & Operations Mgt. Unit Research Paper No. 07–016 (Harvard Business School, 2006).

26. The results obtained by the OECD (Andrews et al., 2015) follow the same trend: the gap between the top 5 and the rest of the economy is growing. According to the authors of that study, the leading firms manage to block the spread of their advances to the rest of the economy.

27. We find the same misunderstanding even farther back in economic history. When the railroads were invented, it was thought they would connect towns and villages to the cities and allow them to participate from a distance in the rapid urban expansion. The opposite happened: the cities devoured the villages. As it happens, railroads, as the economists say, allow you to travel in both directions. Why live in a town if you can live in the city and receive supplies of merchandise from throughout the world?

28. Jeremy Rifkin, *The End of Work* (New York: Putnam's Sons, 1995).

29. Daron Acemoglu and Pascual Restrep "The Race between Man and Machine, *American Economic Review* 108, no. 6 (June 2018): 1488–1542.

30. Joel Mokyr, *The Lever of Riches: Technological Creativity and Economic Progress* (Oxford: Oxford University Press, 1990). On this point, see Acemoglu and Restrepo, "Race between Machine and Man."

31. Autor and Dorn, "The Growth of Low Skill Service Jobs."

32. Timothy Bresnahan and Manuel Trajtenberg, "General Purpose Technologies, Engines of Growth?" *Journal of Econometrics* 65, no. 1 (January 1995).

33. Yann LeCun, *Quand la machine apprend* (Paris: Odile Jacob, 2019).

34. The fundamental article is Bengt Holmstrom and Paul Milgrom's "Multitask Principal-Agent Analyses," *Journal of Law, Economics and Organization* (1991): 24–52. ; see also Maya [Bacache] Beauvallet, *Les stratégies absurdes* (Paris: Seuil, 2009).

Chapter 7: iGen

1. Deleuze and Guattari, *Milles plateaux*.

2. Bruno Patino and Jean-François Fogel, *La condition numérique* (Paris: Grasset, 2013).

3. Nevertheless, Robin Dunbar, an English anthropologist cited by Patino and Fogel and the inventor of "Dunbar's number," has shown there is a (psychological) limit to the size of a human group with which an individual can engage in social life. According to Dunbar, the average size is 148 individuals, which corresponds to the number of members in hunter-gatherer encampments, nomadic tribes, and military units in ancient Rome. Studying interactions on Facebook, Dunbar identified an average of 338 "real" connections. In reality, then, Facebook can double the historic size of human groups.

4. Jean Twenge, *iGen*.

5. According to the surveys Twenge assembled, screen time itself can be divided as follows: 28 percent on texts, 24 percent on the Internet, 18 percent on video games, 24 percent on television, 5 percent on chats.

6. Raphaëlle Bacqué, "Avoir vingt ans en 2018: grandir, drôles de familles," *Le Monde*, March 29, 2018.

7. 36 percent less lonely, 33 percent less depressed, and 9 percent happier. The Danish study was conducted on adults, the American study on college students.

8. Jean Twenge, *iGen*.

9. According to the Well-Being Observatory of CEPREMAP (Centre pour la Recherche Économique et Ses Applications).

10. François Hartog, *Régimes d'historicité* (Paris, Le Seuil, 2003).

11. Aldo Schiavone, *Storia and Destino* (Turin: Einaudi, 2007).

12. Éric Sadin, *La vie algorithmique. Critique de la raison numérique* (Paris: L'Échappée, 2015).

13. Nicholas Negroponte, *Being Digital* (1995), Nicholas Negroponte (New York: Alfred Knopf, 1995).

14. Harari, *Homo deus*.

15. Jean-Pierre Vernant, *L'individu, la mort, l'amour* (Paris, Gallimard, 1996).

16. Anna Mitchell and Larry Diamond, "China's Surveillance State Should Scare Everyone," *Atlantic* February 2, 2018.

17. "Only Miscreants Worry about Net Privacy," interview on CNBC, December 7, 2009.

18. Patino and Fogel list several syndromes attributable to the digital world: attention-deficit disorder, which leads sufferers to pay only superficial attention to multiple sources of information; obsessive compulsive disorder; anxiety disorder, caused by recurring intrusive thoughts that generate compulsive behaviors; and attention-deficit/hyperactivity disorder.

19. Jacques-Alain Miller, "Lacan, idole ou démon de la psychanalyse, mourait il y a 30 ans," *Le Point*, August 18, 2011.

20. As Baudrillard said, "It is no longer a question of imitation or replication or even parody, but of a substitution of the signs of the real for the real." Jean Baudrillard, *Simulacres et simulations* (Paris: Galilée, 1981).

21. Philippe Van Parijs and Yannick Vanderborght, *Basic Income: A Radical Proposal for a Free Society and a Sane Economy* (Cambridge: Harvard University Press, 2017).

22. Thomas Paine, *Agrarian Justice* (Paris: T. Williams, 1797).

23. Antonio Casilli, *En attendant les robots* (Paris: Seuil, 2019).

24. Gorz, *Farewell*.

Conclusion

1. Harari, *Homo deus*.

2. Le Goff, *La France d'hier* (Stock, 2018).

3. Joel Mokyr makes this distinction between Smithian and Schumpeterian capitalism in *The Lever of Riches* (Oxford: Oxford University Press, 1990).

INDEX

abortion, 96–97
Acemoglu, Daron, 122
Action Directe (organization), 45
addictions, 136
affirmative action, 51
Ali, Ayaan Hirsi, 93–94
Ali, Haweya, 94
alienation, 34–35
Althusser, Louis, 23, 29
antitrust laws, 139
Arendt, Hannah, 78–80, 122
Argentina, 69, 87
artificial intelligence, 110–12, 114–17;
    racism in, 131; to reduce global
    warming, 144
artisanal-type workers, 82–83
Ashenfelter, Orley, 51
Askenazy, Philippe, 61, 62, 141
Audier, Serge, 30
Audran, René, 45
Australia, 87
automobiles, 12
Autor, David, 124, 125
avatars (aliases), 137–38

Baader, Andreas, 95–96
Baader-Meinhof gang, 96
Bacqué, Raphaelle, 129
Baker, Josephine, 77
Bannon, Stephen, 74
Bantigny, Ludivine, 19
Barthes, Roland, 11–12
Baudelot, Christian, 19
Baudrillard, Jean, 12, 134, 161n20
Bauhaus, 76–77
Begin, Menachem, 53
Bell, Daniel, 24
Berlin Wall, 67

Berners-Lee, Tim, 109
Besse, Georges, 45
Bettelheim, Bruno, 39
Bezos, Jeff, 109
Blacks, conservatives on, 50–51
Blair, Tony, 58
Bloom, Allan, 56
Blum, Léon, 104
Boltanski, Luc, 22, 23, 62
Borjas, George, 88, 89
Boston (UK), 71–72
Boulhol, Hervé, 33
Bourdieu, Pierre, 20
Bouretz, Pierre, 156n13
Bouyeri, Mohammed, 89–90
Breitbart News (website), 74
Brexit, 71–72
Brin, Sergey, 109
Brynjolfsson, Erik, 120
Burke, Edmund, 2, 56
Buruma, Ian, 89–94
Bush, George W., 62–63

Cailliau, Robert, 109
Calment, Jeanne, 115
Cambridge Analytica (firm), 140
Canada: homicides in, 45–46; immi-
    gration to, 87; violence in, 97
Čapek, Karel, 116
capitalism, 23–24; consumption
    encouraged by, 149; current form
    of, 60–62; deindustrialization
    in, 33; as Faustian bargain, 146;
    Gorz on, 35, 144–45; social dis-
    connection under, 85; Weber on
    origins of, 63
Card, David, 88
Carlos, 96

A NOTE ON THE TYPE

{ornament}

THIS BOOK has been composed in Miller, a Scotch Roman typeface designed by Matthew Carter and first released by Font Bureau in 1997. It resembles Monticello, the typeface developed for The Papers of Thomas Jefferson in the 1940s by C. H. Griffith and P. J. Conkwright and reinterpreted in digital form by Carter in 2003.

Pleasant Jefferson ("P. J.") Conkwright (1905–1986) was Typographer at Princeton University Press from 1939 to 1970. He was an acclaimed book designer and AIGA Medalist.

The ornament used throughout this book was designed by Pierre Simon Fournier (1712–1768) and was a favorite of Conkwright's, used in his design of the *Princeton University Library Chronicle*.